THE WAY OF ST FRANCIS

VIA DI FRANCESCO: FROM FLORENCE TO
ASSISI AND ROME

About the Author

Sanford 'Sandy' Brown is an activist, long-distance walker and ordained minister from Seattle, Washington. After reading *The Pilgrimage* by Paolo Coelho in 1992 he planned his first trek on the Camino de Santiago, and since then has walked over 3500 kilometers on pilgrim trails in Spain and Italy. He records his pilgrim adventures in his popular blog, www.caminoist.org.

Sandy earned his Master of Divinity at Garrett Theological Seminary – which honored him in 2006 as Distinguished Alumnus – and has a degree in medieval history. In 1997 he earned a doctorate from Princeton Theological Seminary in gender, sexuality and spirituality. He was executive director of the Church Council of Greater Seattle and most recently was senior pastor of Seattle's historic First United Methodist Church.

In his spare time Sandy enjoys yoga, sailing and playing piano. He has two grown sons and his life partner, Theresa Elliott, is a yoga master teacher.

THE WAY OF ST FRANCIS

VIA DI FRANCESCO: FROM FLORENCE TO ASSISI AND ROME

by Sandy Brown

2 POLICE SQUARE, MILNTHORPE, CUMBRIA LA7 7PY
www.cicerone.co.uk

Printed by KHL Printing, Singapore.

A catalogue record for this book is available from the British Library.

All photographs are by the author unless otherwise stated.

Route mapping by Lovell Johns www.lovelljohns.com
Contains OpenStreetMap.org data © OpenStreetMap
contributors, CC-BY-SA. NASA relief data courtesy of ESRI

Acknowledgements

A big thanks to Jacqueline Zeindlinger, who pored through German language guidebooks to help me learn more about the route. Thanks to my sister, Lori McCarney and her husband Rick who hosted me as I wrote the proposal. My language school, Comitato Linguistico in Perugia, gave me confidence to speak Italian. The help of several Italians was crucial: Gigi Bettin, The Most Rev Paulo Giulietti, auxiliary bishop of the Perugia Diocese, Salvatore Accardi of Il Mestiere di Viaggiare. Thanks to each of them, along with First United Methodist Church of Seattle that blessed me with a Garmin GPS, and Robin Werner, who lent his excellent Sony NEX-7 camera.

Of course, the book would not have happened without Jonathan Williams of Cicerone. Lois Sparling, Cicerone's Editorial Production Manager, always had helpful insights and Georgia Laval vastly improved the text and its coordination with maps and photos. My walking partner and companion, Theresa Elliott, was a constant and joyful inspiration each step of the way. The book is dedicated to all who hope to find adventure, spirit, and joy in the ancient paths of the Saints.

Front cover: Views down to Spello and the Tiber Valley along the upper trail from Assisi (Stage 16A)

CONTENTS

Updates to this Guide

While every effort is made by our authors to ensure the accuracy of guidebooks as they go to print, changes can occur during the lifetime of an edition. Any updates that we know of for this guide will be on the Cicerone website (www.cicerone. co.uk/626/updates), so please check before planning your trip. We also advise that you check information about such things as transport, accommodation and shops locally. Even rights of way can be altered over time.

The route maps in this guide are derived from publicly-available data, databases and crowd-sourced data. As such they have not been through the detailed checking procedures that would generally be applied to a published map from an official mapping agency, although naturally we have reviewed them closely in the light of local knowledge as part of the preparation of this guide.

We are always grateful for information about any discrepancies between a guidebook and the facts on the ground, sent by email to info@cicerone.co.uk or by post to Cicerone, 2 Police Square, Milnthorpe LA7 7PY, United Kingdom.

Symbols used on route maps

	route
	alternative route
(S)	start point
(F)	finish point
(SF)	start/finish point
<	direction of route
	glacier
	woodland
	urban areas
	international border
	regional border
	station/railway
▲	peak
⋏	campsite
■	building
⚱ †	church/cross
♜	castle
⬆ ⇧	manned/unmanned refuge
∘	water feature
M	metro symbol

Relief

5000 and above
4800–5000
4600–4800
4400–4600
4200–4400
4000–4200
3800–4000
3600–3800
3400–3600
3200–3400
3000–3200
2800–3000
2600–2800
2400–2600
2200–2400
2000–2200
1800–2000
1600–1800
1400–1600
1200–1400
1000–1200
800–1000
600–800
400–600
200–400
0–200

SCALE: 1:50,000

0 kilometres 0.5   1
0 miles   0.5

Contour lines are drawn at 25m intervals and highlighted at 100m intervals.

GPX files

GPX files for all routes can be downloaded for free at www.cicerone.co.uk/member.

The Duomo, tower and main piazza of Spoleto (Stage 19)

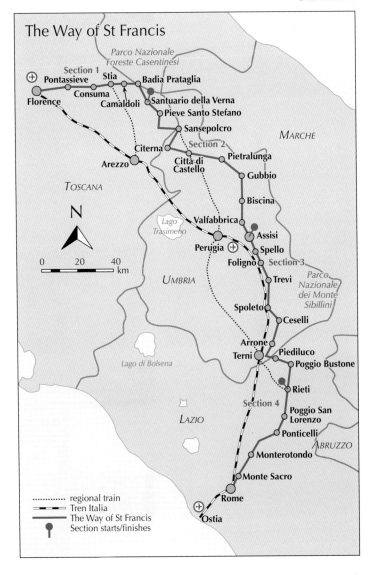

The Way of St Francis

Parco Nazionale
Foreste Casentinesi

Section 1

Pontassieve · Stia · Badia Prataglia
Consuma · Santuario della Verna
Florence · Camaldoli · Pieve Santo Stefano
Sansepolcro

MARCHE

Citerna · Section 2 · Pietralunga
Arezzo · Città di Castello · Gubbio

TOSCANA

N

Biscina

Lago Trasimeno · Valfabbrica

Assisi

Perugia · Spello

0   20   40
km · Foligno · Section 3

UMBRIA · Trevi

Parco Nazionale dei Monte Sibillini

Spoleto

Ceselli

Arrone · Piediluco

Lago di Bolsena · Terni · Poggio Bustone

Rieti

Section 4

LAZIO · Poggio San Lorenzo

Ponticelli · ABRUZZO

Monterotondo

Monte Sacro

Rome

Ostia

.... regional train
━━━ Tren Italia
━━━ The Way of St Francis
● Section starts/finishes

9

Signs in Casentino Park showing trails to nearby mountains (Stage 5)

INTRODUCTION

Vittorio Emanuel II Monument in Rome (Pilgrim Churches Tour)

With your pack on your back you have rounded the last bend of the Tiber River. You have walked past the looming brown hulk of Castel Sant'Angelo, past some offices and stores and, with 140 stern, saintly and stony witnesses watching from the colonnade above, you have stepped out of Italy and into bustling Saint Peter's Square. This is holy ground, the Vatican City – for many the center of the world. After many days of walking you should be exhausted, but instead you're exhilarated.

Before you is Michelangelo's spectacular dome, soaring over the tomb of St Peter. To your upper right is the Pope's balcony where he speaks to tens of thousands of the assembled faithful. Beyond is the treasure-filled Vatican Museum. Behind you are relics of Ancient Rome, its temples and palaces sprinkled within one of the world's most beloved and beautiful modern cities.

Around you are pilgrims from all over the world, here like you to experience the drama and grandeur of this place. They came in a bus or train or car; but like millions of pilgrims from centuries past who spent weeks or months getting to this very place, you walked. You feel your arrival in a joyful heart, but also you feel it in your bones and muscles and on the soles of your weary feet. You take off your pack to rest your back after a journey

Interior of St Peter's Basilica, Rome (Stage 28)

of many kilometers, and with a mixture of relief and joy you think back over your amazing pilgrimage – the Way of St Francis.

Stretching out over 28 days and 550 kilometers, the Via di San Francesco unveils countless unforgettable wonders. In Florence are the smooth, muscular lines of Michelangelo's David, the amazing heights of Brunelleschi's dome, the heavy bells of Giotto's tower and intricate details of Ghiberti's bronze doors. After Florence are countless medieval and Renaissance churches and monuments that stand in timeless testimony to a people's enduring faith over many centuries. In Assisi are delicate frescoes by Cimabue and Giotto. Roman amphitheaters, Etruscan arches and relics of saints dot the path that traces a pilgrim walk through cities and villages but also under the shade of mighty forests and ancient olive groves.

Many have walked to Rome – heroes and conquerors, saints and reformers – but none loved this land more than St Francis of Assisi, a simple man of Umbria who became patron saint of Italy. In his *Canticle of Brother Sun and Sister Moon* he offered a poetic vision for a life that calls people to befriend the earth and all God's creatures. That song and his life sprang from this sun over these fields, these forests, these stones.

The modern Way of St Francis connects places and paths important in the life of this beloved saint and makes them available to pilgrim walkers who seek to retrace his steps and

View of the Basilica of St Francis from Porta San Giacomo (Stage 15)

Street scene near the train station in Florence

capture his love of this land. Indeed, the ministry of Francis of Assisi began with a walk – in 1209 when he and his friends walked from Assisi to Rome to meet Pope Innocent III. His travels north of Assisi and in Tuscany inspire stories told to this day. He loved to visit in the Holy Valley of Rieti for rest and prayer. The Way of St Francis links these travels and destinations into a month-long walk that even after many centuries echoes with his presence.

Today, as you walk from Florence to Rome via Assisi it is easy to imagine the Italy of Francis' time. Still present are the thick, grey-brown walls of medieval hill towns, the quiet mountain pathways, the sweeping vistas of fertile farmland where wheat and herb are grown, and the ancient olive groves where locals know to find the tender stalks of the wild asparagus they gather by hand and toss with the pasta of their evening meal. These Central Apennines contain some of Italy's most beautiful mountains and valleys, what Italians call *il cuor verde d'Italia* – the green heart of Italy.

If the mountains of Umbria, Tuscany and Lazio could speak of all that has happened in their shadow, they would tell a rich and color-ful story of armies and conquerors, of mysterious Etruscans and crafty Romans, of Christian princes and worldly bishops, of invading hordes and bumbling dictators – all who made marks on the land that today are still visible to the observant pil-grim walker. Every day of this walk brings evidence of another historic episode to see and touch: an Umbrian archway, a Roman road, a papal castle, a monument to soldiers lost in a war, a gleaming new European Union highway.

The Way of St Francis lays Central Italy at your feet and dares you not to love it. When you finally arrive in Rome and walk past the Swiss Guard to hand your credential to the man at the desk deep inside the Vatican walls, and are given your completion certificate – your testimonium – your sense of accomplishment will be well-earned, having just completed one of the world's greatest pilgrimages.

But much more than that, you will have joined the countless pilgrims to Rome from over the centuries who've made a special place in their heart for this beautiful land, its deep and rich history, its food and people, and its humble patron saint who walked with you along the way.

ST FRANCIS AND THE WAY OF ST FRANCIS

The life of St Francis of Assisi

When Pietro and his French wife, Pica, celebrated the birth of their son Francis, in about 1181, they undoubtedly expected him to take up the family's prosperous cloth business in Assisi. As an adolescent, when Francis was not helping his father he was perfecting his skills as a horseman, archer and warrior – aristocratic proficiencies

befitting the upper classes to which his family aspired.

In 1202 war broke out between Assisi and neighboring Perugia. Dressed in fine battle gear, Francis boldly joined his countrymen to fight the Perugians, but the tragic result was a heavy loss of life and many casualties in the brief but bloody conflict. The Perugian victors sorted the conquered soldiers between peasants, who were killed, and aristocrats, who were imprisoned for ransom. As a result, Francis spent nearly a year in the dungeons of Perugia while his ransom was arranged. He came back to Assisi in 1203 a very different man.

Yes, the cold and damp dungeon had taken a toll on his health, but it was more likely the traumatic experience of human cruelty that changed his outlook. One day after his release from prison he was riding toward Assisi and came across a leper. The old Francis would have been horrified at such a sight and would have kept his distance, but this time he subdued his revulsion and, out of a newfound compassion, gently kissed the man. Francis was living into a new worldview.

He began to spend more time alone in study, deep contemplation and prayer and encouraged his friends to do the same. One day in 1206, from the crucifix of the ruined church of San Damiano just outside Assisi's walls, he heard these words: 'Francis, rebuild my church.'

'One scene of the life of St Francis in graffiti style on a concrete wall leaving Valfabbrica (Stage 15)

Along with a dozen of his friends he began to do just that. To fund his work Francis chose to tap a familiar source – his family. Without asking permission, Francis availed himself of expensive bolts of cloth from Pietro's stock; he sold them and used the proceeds to help pay for the reclamation project. Needless to say, Pietro was incensed and imprisoned Francis in a basement room of his home. Appealing to Bishop Guido of Assisi against his son, Pietro had Francis put on trial at the town's Santa Maria Maggiore church, and there the bishop ordered Francis to repay his father the cost of the cloth. In a symbolic act of separation, Francis removed his clothes and handed them to his father, renouncing him, his family, their possessions, and their way of life.

In a rough tunic, given him out of pity by the bishop of Assisi, Francis set out for the house of a friend in Gubbio. Over the next two years the small band of friends he had gathered would travel together like roving troubadours – a band of 'brothers' on a quest of prayer, poverty and preaching. They investigated the scriptures at Santa Maria Minerva church in Assisi and there discovered Jesus' call to poverty and simplicity.

With his brothers Francis traveled to Poggio Bustone, where he had a spiritual experience of transformation, and to nearby Lake Piediluco as the band continued to gain attention. The religious authorities in Rome took notice of the growing movement, and in its biggest test, Francis was summoned in 1210 to St John Lateran by

Pope Innocent III to explain his unauthorized gospel ministry.

Aptly remembered as one of the wisest of all popes, Innocent carefully pondered the ragged man in the tattered brown robe before him. Afterwards, in a dream, the pope saw Francis holding up the pillars of his church, which was tottering in an earthquake; shortly after that he gave his blessing and Francis began a preaching mission that would send him across the Western world.

Over the next years literally thousands of men would join his Franciscan order. Soon, women would unite with a second order set up by his friend and confidante, Clare of Assisi. A third order of laypeople would also be formed – propelled by the sincerity, humility and the gentle spirituality of the humble man of Assisi.

Operating from his base at the tiny Porziuncola chapel at Santa Maria degli Angeli below Assisi, his travels would take him to Spain, France, throughout Italy and to the Middle East as a peace-loving adjunct to the Fifth Crusade.

Back in Italy, Francis sought quiet, remote settings for prayer and contemplation – Monteluco, La Verna, Montecasale, Fontecolombo, and many more – all the while gaining fame as stories of miracles surrounded his mission.

Unknown even to his closest friends, at La Verna in 1224 he

Francis Memorial at St John Lateran Cathedral in Rome (photo by Jacqueline Zeindlinger)

received 'stigmata' – marks on his hands, feet and sides resembling Jesus' wounds on the cross. He kept these hidden from others so as not to appear proud.

Because of an ailment to his eyes, in 1225 the Bishop of Rieti begged Francis to come to his town and receive treatment, but the pressing of the crowds forced him to remain outside of town for several weeks at a quiet church of La Foresta. Then, in nearby Greccio, Francis' temples were cauterized from his ears to his eyelids, although Francis insisted he felt no pain.

With his health in continued decline, Francis returned to La Verna, then Montecasale, and finally to Assisi. He visited with his colleague, Clare, and in a hut outside San Damiano he finalized the rule of his order and penned his immortal song, the *Canticle of Brother Sun*.

On 3 October 1226, at the Porziuncola, Francis died, surrounded by weeping followers and thousands of devotees. On his body were discovered the stigmata, which startled his followers and lent added wonder to the multiplying stories and legends of his life. In less than two years he was declared a saint and construction began on a church at Assisi in his honor. At the completion of its lower level, the body of Francis was interred at the new Basilica of San Francesco.

Some have called Francis of Assisi the most successful follower of Jesus Christ, fulfilling in the most

meticulous way Jesus' call to simplicity, poverty and prayer. In practical terms his life, ministry and legacy steered the church back toward care of the poor and needy.

In the 20th century Francis' love of nature led him to be called 'the first environmentalist,' and his interest in the poor has made him informal patron saint of economic justice. Then in 2013 the newly elected Cardinal Jorge Bergoglio of Buenos Aires took the name, Pope Francis. The message was not lost – Bergoglio was saying to people of the 21st century that they should take a fresh look at the life and message of the humble man of Assisi.

(There are many resources for those who would like to learn more about Francis' life and legacy; see Appendix D for further reading suggestions.)

The modern Way of St Francis

After the death of Francis his hometown of Assisi became an important pilgrimage site. Since the 13th century pilgrims from all over Italy and Europe have traveled to Umbria to venerate Francis and his friend and collaborator, St Clare. Today, the Municipality of Assisi annually hosts over 4 million pilgrims and tourists.

Since there is no historic text that proposes a specific itinerary, as with other pilgrimages such as the Camino de Santiago and Via Francigena, there are now several itineraries that link together beloved St Francis sites. Among the main routes are:

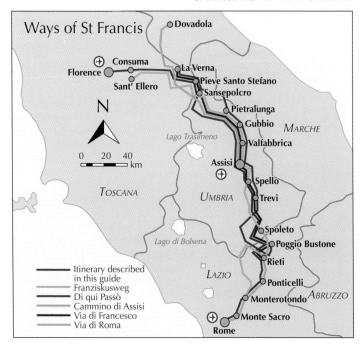

Ways of St Francis

- Dovadola
- Consuma
- Florence
- Sant' Ellero
- La Verna
- Pieve Santo Stefano
- Sansepolcro
- Pietralunga
- Gubbio
- Valfabbrica
- Assisi
- Spello
- Trevi
- Spoleto
- Poggio Bustone
- Rieti
- Ponticelli
- Monterotondo
- Monte Sacro
- Rome

MARCHE
Lago Trasimeno
TOSCANA
UMBRIA
Lago di Bolsena
LAZIO
ABRUZZO

N

0   20   40 km

Itinerary described in this guide
Franziskusweg
Di qui Passò
Cammino di Assisi
Via di Francesco
Via di Roma

- **Via Francigena di San Francesco (Via di Francesco)** – a joint project of the Region of Umbria, Franciscan family of orders in Assisi and the Umbrian Conference of Catholic Bishops. The routes converge on Assisi, beginning either at Santuario della Verna from the north or Rieti from the south. Large blue-and-yellow metal signs and blue-and-yellow painted stripes mark the way.

- **Cammino di Assisi** begins at the tiny town of Dovadola in

Emilia-Romagna and visits sites of St Anthony before connecting at Santuario della Verna for a Franciscan itinerary that ends in Assisi. Green arrows and a dancing 'Tau' figure mark the route.

- **Di qui Passò San Francesco** is the brainchild of pilgrim pioneer Angela Serracchioli and leads from Santuario della Verna to Poggio Bustone. Look for yellow 'Tau' markers and yellow arrows on this route.

- **Cammino di Francesco** is a project of the Rieti tourism

A small shrine honoring pilgrims outside Foligno (Stage 17)

- **Sentiero Francescano della Pace** recounts the route walked by Francis from Assisi to Gubbio after his parents disowned him. Large kiosks mark the route.
- **Der Franziskusweg** – in their guidebooks, authors Kees Roodenburg of Holland and Simone Ochsenkühn of Germany describe a route beginning near Florence and ending just before Rome. An Austrian guidebook also describes a Franziskusweg route from Frankfurt to Rome via La Verna. Before La Verna the route follows pre-existing Club Alpino Italia (CAI) trails, which are marked in painted red-and-white stripes, and then selects from among the Franciscan options to find the most favorable itineraries.

office, which maintains a ring of trails among the holy sites of the Sacred Valley of Rieti in a circular route between Poggio Bustone, Greccio, La Foresta and other Franciscan sanctuaries. Carved wooden signs and X-framed fences mark the route.

- **Via di Roma** is overseen by the Region of Lazio and leads from Rieti to Rome. Its blue-and-yellow signs are almost identical to those of the Via di Francesco. In Rome the route is also marked with images of St Francis and the two keys of St Peter stenciled in yellow paint on sidewalks.

Why this itinerary?
While the different routes offer their own virtues and give pilgrims

Waymarks along the way, including CAI, Qui Passo, Via Francesco and Cammino di Assisi

A group of pilgrims walking to Assisi from Spello (Stage 16)

choices about what sites to visit and how best to enjoy the area, the lack of agreement on a single itinerary does challenge pilgrims who want to find the best choice for their specific pilgrimage.

The itinerary included in this book comes after weighing the pros and cons of each existing route. The goals of this book's itinerary are to provide the strongest possible links to sites identified with the life of St Francis, as well as providing an enjoyable and scenic daily experience. It also seeks to include daily routes that provide access to services and economical overnight lodging. Since travel connections are important, it includes stages that begin and end in locations with air and/or bus transportation.

Pilgrims have physical limits, so another goal was to avoid unnecessarily long, difficult or poorly marked routes. This route honors safety rules and minimizes time on busy auto roads that provide little or no room for pedestrians. It was also important to allow for a one-month timeframe as a natural follow-up to a pilgrim who has finished the Camino Frances and is looking for another memorable pilgrimage experience. (See 'Planning and training', below, for advice on how to shorten your itinerary if time is at a premium and fitness levels are high.)

After weighing the options, this route follows most closely the Via di Francesco and Via di Roma itineraries from Santuario della Verna to Rome, occasionally opting for the other routes when they offer a better option. The primary addition is a walking itinerary from Florence to hard-to-reach Santuario della Verna, which mostly follows the German guidebooks, leading pilgrims through the lovely Casentino Park.

GEOGRAPHY AND CLIMATE

The Apennine range is the thick spine of the Italian peninsula, and the forested Central Apennines form the north and east borders of the route of the Way of St Francis. On the Western slopes of the Central Apennines the primary rivers are tributaries of the Arno and Tiber (Tevere), which catch rainfall from western Tuscany, Umbria and Lazio before flowing into the Tyrrhenian and Ligurian Seas.

Because of this rugged topography, the Way of St Francis is often a challenging walk. Veteran Camino de Santiago pilgrims may compare several of the days to a walk over the Route Napoleon that crosses the Pyrenees. A daily climb and descent of 500 to 1000 meters is not unusual.

Mount Terminillo and other snowy peaks in the Central Apennines create weather patterns that ensure regular rainfall, and the mountain streams and aquifers supply pure water that is bottled and shipped all over Italy at water plants like Cottorella near Rieti. For pilgrims, this environment means that sporadic rain is assured in any season of the year.

Some who haven't visited Central Italy are surprised to discover this

Looking back toward Cantalice (Stage 23)

Month	Florence			Assisi			Rome		
	Avg low temp C/F	Avg high temp C/F	Avg rainfall mm/in	Avg low temp C/F	Avg high temp C/F	Avg rainfall mm/in	Avg low temp C/F	Avg high temp C/F	Avg rainfall mm/in
Jan	1/34	10/50	73/2.9	0/32	8/46	22/0.9	3/37	12/54	103/4.1
Feb	3/37	12/53	69/2.7	2/36	10/50	34/1.3	4/39	13/55	99/3.9
Mar	4/40	15/59	80/3.2	3/37	13/55	33/1.3	5/41	15/59	68/2.7
Apr	7/45	18/65	78/3.1	6/43	17/63	69/2.7	8/46	18/64	65/2.6
May	11/52	23/74	73/2.9	10/50	22/72	56/2.2	11/52	23/73	48/1.9
Jun	14/58	27/81	55/2.2	13/55	26/79	43/1.7	15/59	27/81	34/1.3
Jul	17/63	31/88	40/1.6	15/59	29/84	50/2	17/63	30/86	23/0.9
Aug	17/62	31/87	77/3	16/61	29/84	24/0.9	18/64	30/86	33/1.3
Sept	14/57	26/79	78/3.1	13/55	25/77	84/3.3	15/59	27/81	68/2.7
Oct	10/50	21/70	88/3.5	9/48	19/66	68/2.7	11/52	22/72	94/3.7
Nov	5/41	14/58	111/4.4	5/41	13/55	64/2.5	7/45	16/61	130/5.1
Dec	2/36	10/50	91/3.6	2/36	9/48	72/2.8	4/39	13/55	111/4.4

lovely region has four distinct seasons, with occasional freezing temperatures in the winter as well as very hot temperatures in the summer. Snow is not uncommon at the higher elevations included on this itinerary, with chilly temperatures and more rain in the lowlands. Summers bring the high temperatures expected of Italy, but rainfall averages show why the region remains green.

For pilgrims, the geography and climate offer rewards – breathtaking views from lofty mountain ridges and long walks in ancient forests or among green fields in quiet valleys. But it is also important for pilgrims to plan and prepare well for the challenges ahead.

GETTING THERE

Florence

Florence has a mid-sized international airport that can be reached from major airline hubs in Europe. Upon arrival, pilgrims can share a €20 taxi for the 30-minute ride to the center city or can wait for the VolaInBus – a shuttle to the Santa Maria Novella train station that leaves every 30 minutes (from 5.30am to 1.00am, €6). Santa Maria Novella is the central train station in Florence and is served by trains from all over Europe. Florence's main attractions are all a quick walk from here, as is the Basilica of Santa Croce, start of the pilgrimage.

You can also get to Florence from Rome, whose Fiumicino Airport has excellent connections to cities around the world. A train from the airport to Rome's Termini Station costs €17 and from there the 1hr 30min ride to Florence costs about €19.

Santuario della Verna

Without a car, a trip to La Verna requires a train and/or bus, most often through Bibbiena.

From Florence

By bus, take the Etruria Mobilitá (www.etruriamobilita.it) to Bibbiena, and then transfer to the Pieve Santo Stefano bus to go to Santuario Della Verna. You can also take the train (www.trenitalia.it) from Florence to Arezzo, then transfer to a local TFT train (www.trasportoferro viariotoscano.it) to Bibbiena and take the Etruria Mobilitá bus from there.

From Rome

Take the train to Arezzo, transfer to the TFT train from Arezzo to Bibbiena, and then transfer to the Etruria Mobilitá bus to Santuario della Verna as above.

Assisi

Most travelers to Assisi choose to fly to Florence or Rome and then take the train to Assisi's nearest station, Santa Maria Degli Angeli. From the station there is an hourly €1 bus for the last 2.5km uphill to Assisi. In the daytime it's a 45-minute walk uphill on the 'Pax et Bonum' pedestrian walkway from the train station to Assisi.

Assisi also shares the Aeroporto San Francesco d'Assisi (PEG) with Perugia at Sant'Egidio, about 10km

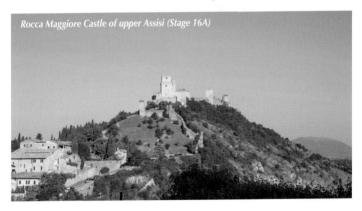

Rocca Maggiore Castle of upper Assisi (Stage 16A)

out of town (www.airport.umbria.it), with direct links to several European cities including London, Dusseldorf, Brussels and Barcelona. Information on the infrequent local bus (number E007) can be found at www. umbriamobilita.it under 'S Egidio Aeroporto', but lack of frequent runs makes it most convenient to pay the approximately €25 cab fare for the 15-minute trip to Assisi.

See Appendix B for a directory of contact details including those of local and national transport providers.

GETTING AROUND

Once in Italy there are relatively economical and simple options for getting around the country.

By train

As with most of Europe, Italy has a good train infrastructure. The TrenItalia system (www.trenitalia.it) serves several stops on the itinerary for this walk, including Florence (Stage 1), Pontassieve (Stage 2), Assisi (Stage 16), Spello (Stage 17), Foligno and Trevi (Stage 18), Spoleto (Stage 19), Rieti (Stage 24) and Monterotondo (Stage 27). TrenItalia tickets are purchased at automated kiosks in train stations and take cash, credit or debit cards (PIN required). They can also be purchased online, although the system requires a membership and identification.

As mentioned above, Tuscany has the small TFT train system (www. trasportoferroviariotoscano.it) that connects Stia (Stage 4) to Bibbiena with its bus connections to Camaldoli and La Verna, plus Arezzo with its TrenItalia station connecting TFT to the main rail network. Tickets are purchased at the station or at nearby tobacco stores or cafés.

Umbria has its FCO system, now run by Umbria Mobilitá (www. umbriamobilita.it) that connects Sansepolcro (Stage 9) and Città di Castello (Stage 11) through Perugia, ending at Rieti (Stage 24). Perugia and Rieti both offer TrenItalia connections. Tickets are purchased at the station.

In Italy, always make certain to validate your ticket by stamping it in the station's validation machine after your purchase or be ready to pay a €40 fine.

By bus

Italy's buses are organized by region, so in Tuscany between Florence (Stage 1) and Sansepolcro (Stage 9) the Etruria Mobilitá system (www. etruriamobilita.it) serves each stop on the itinerary. Umbria Mobilitá (www. umbriamobilita.it) serves the Umbrian portion between Sansepolcro and Piediluco (Stage 22), while Cotral (www.cotralspa.it) serves the Lazio portion from Poggio Bustone (Stage 23) to Rome (Stage 28). Bus schedules are usually posted at each bus stop, and tickets can be purchased from the driver. Bring coins for exact change (usually in the €2–3 range) and always remember to stamp your ticket in the validation machine behind the driver's seat.

Appendix B includes contact details for each region's public transport providers.

May, June, July, September and October are the best months to walk the Way of St Francis. During these months the temperatures range from mild to hot and the rainfall is at its lowest.

The month of August – particularly its last weeks – is best avoided. For the last 2000 years Italians have celebrated Ferragosto – a two-week holiday at the end of August when Italians close their shops and retreat to the mountains and beaches. It is not unusual for small businesses and restaurants to be closed the entire month, so an August walk could mean spotty services along the way.

Due to the winter climate of the highlands and the likelihood of heavy rain and snow, a pilgrimage between December and February on certain portions of the Way of St Francis is unwise. The possibility of trail washouts and signage lost due to snow – not to mention the danger of hypothermia and getting lost – seem unnecessary gambles. Likewise, walking in the shoulder months of October/November and March/April can mean that some places are not yet open for the season.

Pilgrims may want to coordinate their journey around special holidays in the Italian communities on the pilgrimage. Gubbio's Corsa dei Ceri is held on 15 May each year, and Spello's Infiorata lands on the ninth Sunday after Easter. Near Assisi are Perugia's Umbria Jazz in

The Piazza and tower in Valfabbrica (Stage 14)

26

July and EuroChocolate in October, and Spoleto's Due Mondi in June/July attracts classical artists from around the world. Although the festivals are a real treat, pilgrims should be aware that accommodation might be scarce without adequate advance reservations.

ACCOMMODATION

Stages have been arranged to coincide with lodging availability. Where possible, at least three accommodation options are listed per daily stage. The daily listings include low-cost hotels, agriturismi, and *foresterie* (guest houses), followed by at least one hostel, if available. Where possible the address, phone number (exclusive of the +039 prefix for Italy), email address and price for a single and double room are included.

Wherever you stay, it is important to plan ahead and make a reservation, whether you use hotels, agriturismi or hostels. Make your reservations at least 2–3 days ahead so you know you'll have a suitable place to stay. Hostels often do not use email and phone is the only option. Try not to make reservations more than 4–5 days ahead so you maintain some flexibility in your plans.

See Appendix B (Useful contacts) for a stage-by-stage list of tourist information offices; if you find yourself struggling to make a booking they may be able to help.

Hostels

In the larger cities, a youth hostel – *ostello* – is always available. In smaller towns along the route, many parishes or convents open up spare rooms for use by pilgrims. A sleeping bag is not required since virtually every hostel makes linens available for free or for a small cost (except as noted).

Rifugios

These are mountain huts found in national parks (such as the Casentino) and they are maintained by the local chapters of the Club Alpino Italia (CAI). Extremely basic, there may simply be a bare cot, table and fireplace and no restaurant nearby. With only one rifugio along the way – just after Camaldoli – it's likely not worth it to plan to stay there since an overnight would require a sleeping bag, food, cooking utensils and a gas stove.

Agriturismi

An *agriturismo* is a rural guesthouse, with eating accommodations that range from small dining rooms with prepared meals to apartments with kitchens. An overnight at an agriturismo with breakfast and dinner can be in the €70–90 range, and if it is remotely located there may be no other dining options. It's always best to check in advance about the eating options so you can make the meal choice that best meets your budget. In a few cases this means opting out of the agriturismo dinner in favor of a walk or hitched ride to a nearby restaurant.

27

Hotels

Hotels in Italy almost always include a continental-style breakfast. Those featured in this guide usually range from €30–50 per person per night. Reduce the cost by sharing a double room with a trusted friend. Expect to be asked for your passport when you check in, but not to pay until you check out; if you plan to leave early in the morning, ask to pay the night before. And don't forget to pick up your passport before you leave.

Foresterie

A *foresteria* is a hotel run by a convent or monastery (such as Camaldoli and La Verna) that offers hotel-like rooms with breakfast and a one-menu dinner included in the price.

Camping

While it is possible to camp, you would need a tent or other gear for outdoor sleeping which would mean unnecessary extra weight.

EATING IN ITALY

An espresso with perhaps a croissant (*cornetto* in Italian) is an Italian breakfast. Lunch is served in early afternoon and is followed by the *riposo* (see 'Business hours and the riposo', below). Early evening is time for a snack – a glass of beer or wine with tiny bites of food. Although restaurants generally open around 7.00pm, Italians usually enjoy dinner from around 8.00pm until 10.30pm. Restaurants often are open until midnight, although the kitchen may close sooner. Efficiency-loving Northern Europeans and Americans may need to learn the 'slow food' pattern of Italian restaurant meals, where the kitchen expects you to take your time enjoying food, wine and conversation.

Pizza and pasta are, of course, omnipresent in Italy. However, almost every town has its special take on pasta, and you will endear yourself to your server by ordering the local specialty. In Tuscany and Umbria, beef and pork are highly prized and the many varieties of cured meats are famous the world over.

Even in a plain-looking restaurant a full Italian meal can be expensive, so if you're on a budget (or simply can't eat that much food) feel free to pick and choose from any of the courses. If you do, the server will want to know in what order you'd like your food.

BUDGETING AND CASH

If you're on a tight budget, plan ahead to take advantage of private and parochial hostels. If you prefer to stay in hotels you can save a lot of money by having a companion or two to share the cost. You can cut down on food expense by shopping for your lunch at a grocery store the night before. Only occasionally will you find a room or hostel with a kitchen, so you'll want to learn to study restaurant menus carefully for the most economical choices.

A moderate daily budget per person in double hotel rooms will look something like this:

- Breakfast (incl. with room)
- Lunch €6.00
- Dinner €15.00
- Overnight €30.00
- Incidentals €5.00
- Total €56.00

When it comes to cash, rather than bringing a large stash of Euros it's easiest to have an ATM card with you to get cash from your bank account as needed. Check with your bank to see what the fees are, whether there's a maximum daily withdrawal, and to make sure you're getting a favorable exchange rate. It's also a good idea to bring a second ATM card so you have a backup. A credit card is usually best for hotel reservations.

POST, PHONES AND INTERNET

Italy's state-owned, **public postal service**, Poste Italiane, has offices in towns and cities throughout the country, usually with an ATM outside.

To make accommodation reservations in real time it's very handy to have a **telephone** – and even more handy to have a smart phone with internet capability for email. If you have a smart phone, contact your carrier prior to departure to ask for an international voice and data plan. If this is too expensive – and if your smart phone is unlocked from your local carrier – you can purchase a pre-paid Italian SIM card on arrival in Italy at the office of one of the major carriers (TIM, Vodaphone, WIND, for example). The clerk will install a new card for you and offer you voice and data plans. Make certain to retain your old SIM card so you can use it back home when you return. For international calling remember Italy's country code is +39.

If you do have a smart phone, you can save on the cost of cell-based data by using the **wi-fi** capability of your phone when it's available, as it frequently is in public establishments in cities and towns throughout Italy.

As with most of the world, Italian electricity operates at 220v. With the dawn of international electronic appliances, most phones, cameras and computers have a 110/220v transformer built into the 'power brick'. This means that only a plug adapter is necessary for those coming to Italy from places that use 110v or non-Euro plugs.

BUSINESS HOURS AND THE RIPOSO

Northern Europeans and Americans are often surprised to find Italian stores and businesses closed midday. This is the *riposo*, the mid-afternoon rest observed in much of Italy. If you live in Italy during the summer you'll see the purpose of this custom – the Italian sun can be excruciatingly hot in the mid-afternoon. Businesses typically close around 1.30pm and reopen around 4.30–5.30pm, once the day has cooled off.

There is a sort of weekly riposo, too: stores often close on Saturday at noon and then won't reopen until Monday afternoon or even Tuesday morning.

LAUNDRY

In large cities there are almost always coin-operated Laundromats. Ask the hotel or hostel clerk for the nearest location. Laundry is most reliably washed in the sink, so plan to have soap, clothespins and a clothesline with you.

PLANNING AND TRAINING

Choosing a schedule

While the complete walk of 28 stages with the extra walking tour of Rome could be accomplished in 29 walking days, that's not nearly enough time to enjoy and appreciate this important pilgrimage and its many wonders. Unless you have already toured Rome and Florence you would want to spend at least one or two extra days in each. You can't enjoy Assisi in what's left of the day it took to walk there, so add another day for St Francis' home town. It's good to allow for a day of rest every week anyway, so that means a realistic, complete itinerary would be in the realm of 35 days, not including travel to and from Italy.

If a journey of 35 days is unmanageable, the journey could be broken into several parts to be completed as and when time permits:

- Florence to Assisi – 15 or more days
- La Verna to Assisi – 9 or more days
- Assisi to Rieti – 8 or more days
- Assisi to Rome – 14 or more days

The town and lake of Piediluco with the Castello di Luco above (Stage 21)

A faster schedule?

For those who would like to complete the pilgrimage in one trip, and who are fit enough to undertake longer days than are given in the 28-day itinerary described in this book, it is possible to combine shorter stages and reduce the itinerary to **23 days**. This would involve combining Stages 4 & 5; 9 & 10; 13 & 14; 16, 17 & 18; and 19 & 20 of the longer itinerary, and it would require a daily walking average of 23.7km as opposed to 19.5km, with stages as follows:

Stage	From/to	Distance (km)
1	Firenze/Pontassieve	23.8
2	Pontassieve/Consuma	17.8
3	Consuma/Stia	17
4	Stia/Badia Prataglia	25
5	Badia Prataglia/La Verna	17.5
6	La Verna/Pieve St Stefano	15.2
7	Pieve St Stefano/Sansepolcro	25
8	Sansepolcro/Città di Castello	32.8
9	Città di Castello/Pietralunga	29.8
10	Pietralunga/Gubbio	26.5
11	Gubbio/Biscina	22.7
12	Biscina/Assisi	29.3
13	Assisi/Foligno	19
14	Foligno/Spoleto	33
15	Spoleto/Arrone	30.8
16	Arrone/Piediluco	14.5
17	Piediluco/Poggio	21.8
18	Poggio/Rieti	17.7
19	Rieti/Poggio San Lorenzo	21.8
20	Poggio San Lorenzo/Ponticelli	23.2
21	Ponticelli/Monterotondo	29.8
22	Monterotondo/Monte Sacro	19.3
23	Monte Sacro/Rome	15.4
Total		**528.4**

Bear in mind, however, that longer days will reduce your scope for exploring and appreciating the places along the way. This would be a particular shame at Città di Castello (Stage 8 of the above itinerary), Spello and Trevi (within Stages 13 and 14 above) and, of course, Assisi (Stage 12 above), where you should ensure adequate time the next day for a full tour.

For accommodation options in Foligno, see Stage 17 of the 28-day itinerary, which passes through this lovely medieval town; all other overnights on the shortened itinerary are featured as such in this book.

Training

It's helpful to train in advance of the walk, and this should be part of your careful preparation. Most people are concerned about the cardio fitness aspects of training, but an active person within an average weight range with no hip or knee problems should not find it necessary to do additional cardio training for this walk. After all, if you become winded you can slow down, and the best cardio training comes in the first days of the walk itself.

People who are significantly overweight and have a hard time climbing a stairway or hill will have a difficult time. Likewise, because of the frequent and sometimes steep hills, people with knee or hip problems will find this a difficult walk.

Most important in the training regime is having certainty that your

feet and boots get along well with each other. You should plan to test your boot/sock combination with a few long walks before you leave, preferably in varied terrain, so blisters along the way won't sideline you. Too many pilgrims try to push ahead with untested boots and socks and then develop agonizing blisters that can be serious enough to end their trip. Resolve boot and sock issues before you leave home.

Pilgrim credenziale and testimonium

As well as booking your travel arrangement to Italy it is important to secure your credential (or *credenziale* – a pilgrim 'identity card') within two months of your departure. (This is also a good time to reserve your overnight accommodation for the first couple of stages.)

Pilgrims need a credential to certify their status and to receive a testimonium completion certificate at the end of the walk. This guide recommends the credential of the Via di Francesco because of its many institutional sponsors. The credential is free, but a donation is requested to cover the cost of postage. If you are not in the EU it is easiest to ask your bank to make a check for you in Euros to 'Basilica Papale di Santa Maria degli Angeli.' Download the PDF form from www.viadifrancesco.it or request a form at least two months in advance from info@viadifrancesco.it. After filling it out, scan it and send it (or mail it with your check if possible) to:

Pilgrim cross at the top of the ridge, just before the first view of the Basilica of St Francis on Stage 15

Basilica Papale di Santa Maria
degli Angeli
Ufficio Informazioni
Piaza Porziuncola 1
06088 Santa Maria degli Angeli
(PG)
ITALY

Once you have your credential, keep it safe and dry while you are walking and have it stamped each day at the front desk where you spend the night. Plan ahead carefully so there are adequate blank spots on the credential to last your entire walk.

A completion certificate (*testimonium* in Latin) is offered at the Basilica di San Francesco for those who walk at least 100km to Assisi, and a separate one is offered at the Vatican for those who walk at least 140km to Rome. To receive your testimonium in Assisi, go to the car gate just to the left of the lower entrance of the Basilica, present your credential and ask to be directed to 'Statio Peregrinorum' (the pilgrim office) for your testimonium. To receive a testimonium in Rome, follow the steps listed at the end of Stage 28 in this guidebook.

WHAT TO TAKE

The first rule of packing for a long hike is to have exactly the right amount of gear – and no more. The second rule is never bring anything made of cotton – it's cold when wet and takes too long to dry. Keeping those rules in mind, here is a recommended gear list that works for summer. Heavier clothes are required, of course, in spring and fall.

- **Backpack** – 35-liter size is fine for the average build
- **Backpack rain cover**
- **Emergency foil blanket** – basic survival gear and a must for all outdoor hikes in case of an injury or unintended overnight
- **Hiking shorts** – 1 or 2 pairs
- **Long pants** – lightweight and quick-drying for rain and suitable for churches and restaurants – 1 pair
- **Technical t-shirts** – 2 short sleeve, 1 long sleeve (jogging shirts work nicely)
- **Shirt or blouse (with collar for men)** – 1 for dinner and/or church
- **Underwear** – shorts/panties and bras (stretch poly material for quick dry) – 2 or 3 pairs
- **Socks** – wool trekking socks, light for summer, heavier for cool weather – 3 pairs
- **Sock liners** – 3 pairs for blister prevention
- **Hiking boots** – heavy, tall boots with the thickest possible soles are best in the sometimes mountainous terrain
- **'Camp shoe'** – comfortable, for evenings and walking about town
- **Rain jacket** – of breathable material such as Gore-Tex®
- **Warm layer fleece or light down jacket**
- **Sun/rain hat** – wide brim to protect face, ears and back of the neck from sun exposure

- **Toiletries and toiletry bag** – toothbrush, etc
- **Multi-purpose soap** – one small bar of soap works in the shower and also for hand-washing laundry
- **Camera, camera pouch and charger**
- **Phone and charger**
- **CamelBak® or similar water bladder or other water storage** – 2L (spring/fall) or 3L (summer). Lack of fountains along the way means it's important to bring an adequate water container.
- **Clothespins and clothesline**
- **Passport, airline ticket, waterproof bag for documents**
- **Sunblock lotion**
- **Pen and paper and/or journal**
- **Blister kit** – blisters need prompt attention. Plan to bring the ingredients necessary to treat your blisters before they damage your pilgrimage.
- **Toilet paper roll in a plastic bag**
- **Debit/credit card(s)**
- **Copies of important documents** – scans or hard copies of your passport, travel arrangements and credit/debit cards are priceless in case of theft or loss of the originals.
- **Walking poles** – many pilgrims swear by these to help with balance and to take weight off the knees and hips
- **Swimsuit** – it's lightweight, and you'll miss it if your lodging includes a pool.

- **Mosquito repellant** –very helpful in a few swampy areas.

Layers are the key to staying warm on cold days. With this list, here is your cold weather set-up: 1) technical long sleeve t-shirt closest to the body; 2) fleece or down jacket layer for warmth; 3) rain jacket on top. Add or subtract layers depending on the temperature.

MAPS, GPS AND WAYMARKING

It would be difficult if not impossible to source and then carry the paper maps required to cover the entire route. Detailed Italian hiking maps are hard to come by, and, besides, a comprehensive coverage would involve a great many individual sheets – too many, indeed, to make it a practical option.

Although walking directions are given in great detail in this guide, and each stage includes a 1:50,000 'overview' map, it may ease worries to have a GPS or GPS smartphone application for additional help. GPX tracks for the entire walk can be downloaded at www.cicerone.co.uk. Additionally, nearly all the trails covered in this guide are included in Open Cycle Maps (www.opencyclemap.org), which can be downloaded onto a GPS at very little cost.

Italy has an extensive system of hiking trails, and often the route follows portions of this network. Maintained by volunteers of the Club Alpino Italiano (CAI), the trails are marked in horizontal red-and-white stripes, often with the trail number superimposed in black marker. In this book, all references to CAI trails in walking directions refer to the red-and-white striped markings. CAI trails are usually identified in Open Cycle Maps, which makes it an excellent base map resource for GPS users.

For details of the different pilgrimage waymarkers you will encounter along the Way, see 'The modern Way of St Francis', above.

USING THIS GUIDE

The same pattern of information is given for each of the daily stages specified in this guide. The guide also shares brief information about cities, and stories from the life of St Francis relating to Franciscan sites you will encounter. The book's print format has intentionally been kept very small in order to fit easily into a rucksack.

Maps are provided for each stage, covering 20–30km in a small format – they are intended as overviews rather than step-by-step guidance. Also provided are elevation profiles, which have been generated using GPS information to provide a visual preview of the stage's topography.

An information box at the start of each stage gives the day's essential statistics: start and finish points, distance, total ascent and descent, difficulty rating, duration and any relevant notes. All distances, elevations and durations come from actual experience and were recorded by GPS to help

walkers know their progress during the stage. Stages are rated as 'Easy,' 'Moderate' or 'Hard' based on a rating of climbs, descents and distance.

A brief introduction to the day's walk is then given, and this is followed by a detailed route description, in which places along the way that are also shown on the stage maps are highlighted in **bold** to aid navigation. In most stages the walk directions are very specific because sometimes waymarks and signage are absent or poorly maintained.

Each daily stage features in its description at least 2–3 inexpensive options and a hostel where available. Telephone numbers are included for each, along with email addresses where possible.

At the end of the book, Appendix A provides a look-up table for the stages and distances of this 28-day itinerary; Appendix B comprises a list of contacts that may be of use and interest to visitors, both in planning and during the pilgrimage; and Appendix C gives some handy tips for understanding and being understood in Italian.

Entire books have been written about the sights that are described here in only a few sentences; the reader will hopefully understand that space limitations allow only brief summaries of what are the often quite complicated and profound sights on this walk. Appendix D contains a list of further reading that the pilgrim may find enlightening before, during and after their pilgrimage.

DISCOVERING FLORENCE

Basilica Santa Croce

Birthplace of the Renaissance, Florence is one of the world's most beloved cities. In the daytime it is filled with tourists from around the world who want to see Michelangelo's 'David' and marvel at the dome of Brunelleschi. After dark, if you know where to go, Florence buzzes with nightlife. The town is worthy of several days' discovery, but it's also possible to enjoy its highlights in a very short time.

The center of Renaissance Florence is the Duomo. Starting from **Santa Maria Novella train station**, go south, keeping Santa Maria Novella Church on your right. Follow the Via Panzani and turn left on Via dei Cerretani. From here it is just three blocks to the **Duomo complex**, which includes the San Giovanni Baptistery, Giotto's Tower (Campanile di Giotto), and the Duomo (Cathedral of Santa Maria del Fiore).

Begin at the 14th-century Giotto's Tower where, in the ground floor gift shop, you can purchase a €10 ticket to visit all three adjacent monuments. Climb the steps to the top of the tower and enjoy the beautiful view as well as the tower's set of enormous bells – the oldest of which was cast in 1705. Their melodious cacophony is most dramatic just before Sunday's main

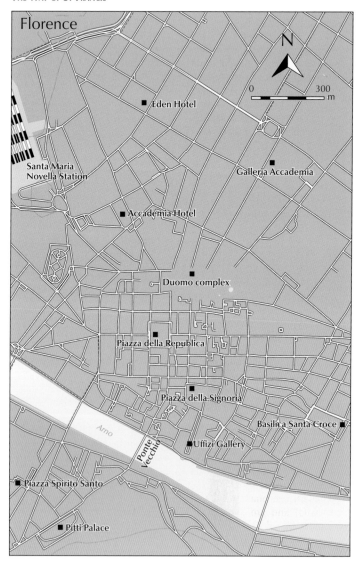

Florence

N

0   300
         m

Eden Hotel

Galleria Accademia

Santa Maria
Novella Station

Accademia Hotel

Duomo complex

Piazza della Republica

Piazza della Signoria

Basilica Santa Croce

Arno

Ponte Vecchio

Uffizi Gallery

Piazza Spirito Santo

Pitti Palace

mass and can be heard for many miles around.

After the tower, visit the Duomo, Florence's colorful cathedral, with Brunelleschi's dome, an engineering marvel of the Renaissance. An interior stairwell allows hardy tourists to reach a spectacular view at the cupola level. The less ambitious can marvel at the frescoes in the ceiling of the dome, the centerpiece of an otherwise relatively plain interior. Arrive early (the Duomo is open 10.00am to 5.00pm except holidays) to avoid the long lines in tourist season, or plan to attend mass which is offered several times each day and allows free access via the south transept.

Across the narrow piazza is the octagonal Baptistery of San Giovanni (built in the 11th–12th century), Florence's oldest religious building and an important example of Florentine Romanesque style. Its bronze doors were added in the 14th–15th century (two sets by Ghiberti and one by Pisano) and are themselves prized art pieces. Michelangelo called Ghiberti's east

doors, 'The Gates of Paradise'. The ceiling is adorned with a spectacular mosaic, the earliest portions of which are attributed to the artist Cimabue.

Standing between the Duomo and the Baptistery, head south along Via dei Calzaiuoli. In two blocks you

The dome of the Duomo, as seen from the tower (Campanile di Giotto)

can catch a view of the touristy **Piazza della Republica** on the right, and in another five blocks you arrive at the **Piazza della Signoria**, with its crenellated and towered Palazzo Vecchio – Florence's town hall. A copy of Michelangelo's 'David' stands in front of the palace, while other impressive but less famous Renaissance statues adorn the square.

Just past the Palazzo Vecchio is the renowned **Uffizi Gallery**, home to treasures of the Middle Ages and Renaissance. 'Birth of Venus' by Botticelli and 'Doni Tondo' (Holy Family) by Michelangelo stand out in the Uffizi's elite collection.

The Uffizi's southern walls face the Arno River; turn right along the river and walk three blocks to the beloved **Ponte Vecchio** (Old Bridge) with its glittering jewelry shops. If you have time, continue across the bridge onto Via de Guicciardini and walk two long blocks to the **Pitti Palace**, which features paintings of Rafael, or turn right across from the palace on Sdrucciolo de Pitti and walk four blocks to the domed Church of Santo Spirito. Enjoy a quiet lunch or dinner in the **Piazza Santo Spirito**, where you can find a hint of less-touristic Florentine life.

Return to central Florence by the Ponte Vecchio and just after the bridge turn right onto the promenade along the Arno. After eight blocks turn left at the next bridge and then right again on Borgo Santa Croce.

Home to the tombs of Michelangelo, Galileo, Machiavelli and many other notable Italians, **Basilica Santa Croce** is arguably Florence's most beautiful worship space. Important Gaddi and Giotto frescoes adorn its ceilings and the adjacent Franciscan convent houses clothing and other relics of St Francis. A €5 admission fee allows entry during its 9.30am–5.00pm hours (Monday–Saturday; 1.00pm–5.00pm on Sunday). The basilica offers a credential stamp in its bookstore, just off the right side of the nave.

From the west side of Piazza Santa Croce follow the Stage 1 route, taking a right along Via Giuseppe Verdi and a left onto Via degli Alfani. Turn right in four long blocks onto Via Ricasoli and in a half block come to the **Accademia Gallery**, home to Michelangelo's 'David.' Plan to make a reservation in advance, then arrive 30 minutes prior (www.uffizi.com).

After a busy day of monuments and museums, enjoy a pleasant evening stroll through the Piazza della Signoria or the Piazza della Republica. For restaurants with typical Tuscan dishes, though, leave the tourists behind and go a block or two off the main track where adventures in typical Italian dining await. Ask for the *zuppa di cipole* (onion soup) or the *pappa al pomodoro* (bread and tomato soup). The bold can try *trippa al Fiorentina* (tripe) for a main course, or perhaps a *bistecca Fiorentina* – the famous local version of the classic T–bone steak.

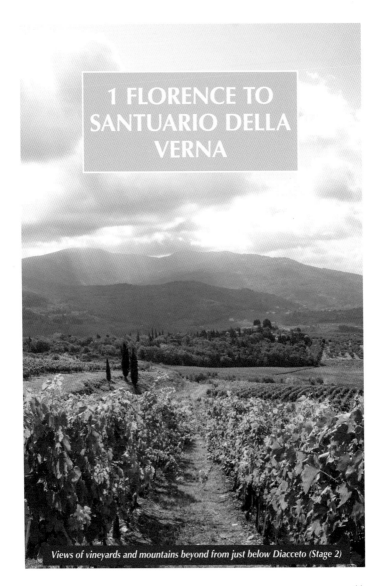

1 FLORENCE TO SANTUARIO DELLA VERNA

Views of vineyards and mountains beyond from just below Diacceto (Stage 2)

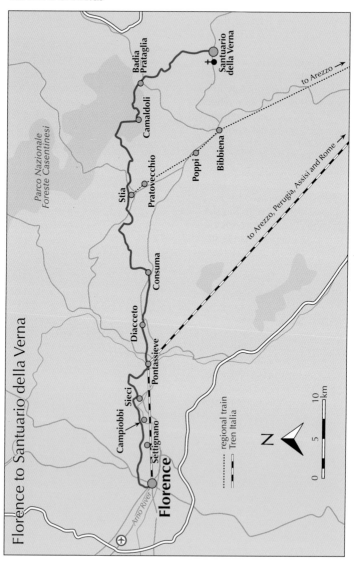

Florence to Santuario della Verna

Santuario della Verna

to Arezzo

Badia Prataglia

Camaldoli

Bibbiena

Poppi

to Arezzo, Perugia, Assisi and Rome

Pratovecchio

Stia

Consuma

Diacceto

Pontassieve

Campiobbi

Sieci

Settignano

Florence

Arno River

Parco Nazionale
Foreste Casentinesi

N

regional train
Tren Italia

0   5   10
km

Standing at the edge of the Late Middle Ages, a time of the dominion of religion and the Church, Michelangelo and his fellow artists looked within Biblical stories for the classic and timeless beauty in their subjects. Their work gave rebirth to the Classical Era, and foreshadowed the Enlightenment and its love of science and nature.

The walk from Florence to Santuario della Verna reverses that progression, as pilgrims walk back in time from the Renaissance into the medieval world of faith. This six-day part of the Way of St Francis carries the walker from the marble statues and frescoed vaults of Florence to remote mountain retreats where centuries earlier reclusive monks, nuns and friars tamed their inner demons to find union with their Creator. The goal, Santuario della Verna, is a mountaintop retreat held dear by St Francis, who loved it for its seclusion.

In Stage 2 comes the moment of transition: turning away from the cultivated vineyards and olive groves of the Arno River Valley at Diacceto, the path takes the pilgrim directly ahead into the deep forests of the looming Central Apennine mountain range. The cultured walls of Renaissance Florence fade into memory as the pilgrim meets the friendly solitude of nature, so prized by mystics.

The route climbs up mountains and down into valleys, all within the drainage of the Arno and its tributaries. After Pontassieve the settlements are mostly mountain hamlets, with Stia and its neighbor, Pratovecchio, the largest towns. From Consuma onward each village on the itinerary serves in some form as a gateway to the vast Casentino National Park and Forest, whose 826 square kilometers of forests and mountains are carefully managed by the Italian government. These rugged woodlands are home to diverse plants and wildlife, including deer, wolves, and wild boar.

Recreational tourists far outnumber pilgrim walkers on these mountain trails, but pilgrims benefit from an infrastructure of economical lodging, relatively plentiful restaurants and shops, and most of all, good trails. The route at times treads portions of other important trail routes – the Grande Escursione Appenninica, the Sentiero Italia, the Cammino di San Vicino, and the lush and beautiful Sentiero delle Foreste Sacre near La Verna.

Hermits, monks and friars – travelers along the active and cloistered walks toward God – can be found along these trails at two of Italy's most revered religious communities. Eremo Camaldoli has been home to monks for nearly 1000 years, while this part's end point, Santuario della Verna, is an active Franciscan community inaugurated by St Francis himself. Pilgrims may want to plan an extra night here to enjoy Franciscan hospitality, visit the many chapels and monuments, and spend extra hours in contemplation at one of Italy's most holy sites.

STAGE 1
Florence to Pontassieve

Start	Basilica of Santa Croce, Florence
Finish	Piazza Vittorio Emanuele II, Pontassieve
Distance	23.8km
Total ascent	602m
Total descent	553m
Difficulty	Easy
Duration	7hrs
Note	Santa Croce doesn't open until 9.30am so you should visit its bookshop the day before to acquire the stamp for your credential.

Memories of Renaissance masterpieces fade quickly as this stage travels through Florence's tony suburbs into green hills, vineyards, olive groves, and along quiet bends of the scenic Arno River.

FLORENCE 50M POP 367,796

Florence's many works of art and culture deserve additional study beyond the scope of this book. If you have never visited Florence, plan at least 1–2 days to enjoy its sites with a good guide or guidebook.

Make your way from the most common entry point – Santa Maria Novella train station – to the starting point of the first stage of the Way of St Francis at the Basilica Santa Croce. As well as being the largest Franciscan church in the world, the Basilica Santa Croce is sometimes called the 'mausoleum of Italy' since it contains the tombs of some of Italy's most revered citizens. The basilica itself is darker and more dense with color than its more famous sibling, the Duomo of Florence. Spend time here to enjoy the ornate tombs and rich frescoes. Entry costs €5 and visiting time is from 9.30am–5.00pm Monday to Saturday, and 1.00pm–5.00pm Sunday. Watch for closures on special holidays. A lovely pilgrim stamp (*timbro*) is available at the bookshop inside the main basilica.

As one of Italy's main tourist destinations, Florence has hundreds of hotels. Two on the lower end of the price scale and near the train station are the recently

renovated Hotel Eden (Via Nazionale 55, tel 055 483722, info@hoteleden.
firenze.it, €50/60, breakfast included) and Hotel Accademia (Via Faenza 7, tel
055 293451, info@hotelaccademiafirenze.com, €50/55, breakfast included).
Florence also has several hostels, but most convenient is the Ostello Villa
Camerata (Viale Augusto Righi 4, tel 055 601451, Firenze@aighostel.it, €15 plus
€2 membership, breakfast available), which despite being 4km from the Santa
Maria Novella train station is on the Stage 1 route. Popular among pilgrims is 7
Santi Hostel (Viale dei Mille 11, tel 055 5048452, info@7santi.com, from €19),
set in a former monastery.

With your back to the Basilica Santa Croce, walk for-
ward through Piazza Santa Croce and at its end turn right
onto Via Giuseppe Verdi. Follow this street, and when it
ends at Via dei Pilastri, turn left. The road immediately
becomes Via degli Alfani, which you follow for about five
blocks until you turn right on Via Ricasoli. Immediately
on the right are queues at the Galleria Accademia for
Michelangelo's David.

Continue past the piazza on the left and come to
busy Viale Matteotti. Turn left here and before you in one
block is leafy **Piazza della Libertà**. Cross into the piazza,
and keeping the 18th-century triumphal arch on your left,
cross the street and take Viale Minzoni, which is just to
the right of a tangerine-and-yellow building. Follow this
tree-lined street for six blocks until the railroad tracks,
which you cross in the pedestrian underpass.

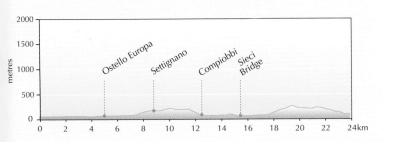

45

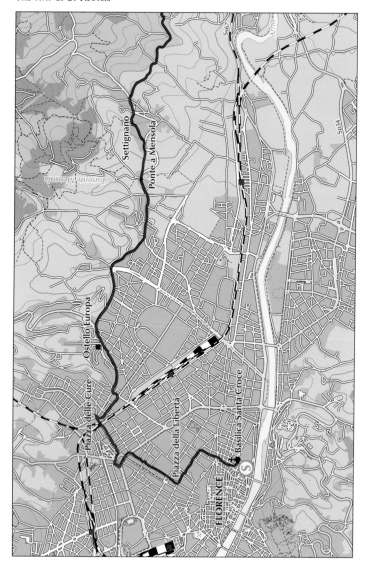

At the fork at the end of the underpass tunnel, turn right and climb the stairs to the east side of **Piazza delle Cure**. Follow the bike path before you along Viale dei Mille for three blocks. Turn left at the third block and then turn right in just one block onto Viale Volta. Walk along this street for 1km until you reach Piazza Edison, a small park, and then turn right at the fork onto Viale Righi. The park and gardens of Villa Il Ventaglio are on the left.

In 1km come to **Ostello Europa** Villa Cameratta on the left (5km) and just afterward cross the Via Lungo l'Affrico straight ahead onto Via del Cantone. Walk along the road for the next 450m, at first with its tall stone wall on the left, until the road ends at Via Fiesole. Turn left and in 250m turn left again when this road ends at Via D'Annunzio. In 800m come to the little village of **Ponte a Mensola** (6.6km). ▶

You are now beyond the outskirts of Florence and entering into the rich olive groves and vineyards of the surrounding countryside, known for its Chianti wines.

Go through the village and look for house number 189 on the left. Just afterward turn left and climb an old stairway, the first steps of Via Vecchia di Settignano. At the top of the steps a grassy road leads uphill toward a large house with a castle-like tower. Turn left at the

Triumphal arch at the Piazza della Libertà

47

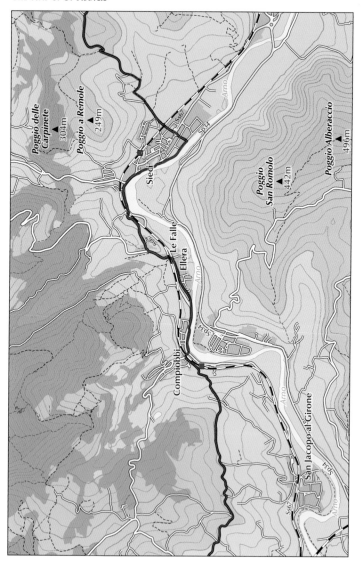

asphalt road passing in front of the house and immediately turn left again, onto Via dei Ceci.

As you walk uphill, notice in 300m a wide path going more steeply uphill to the right. Take the path and arrive at Piazza Desiderio. Go straight past the imposing statue and continue on Via Mosca for 200m to the main piazza of **Settignano** (7.6km) with its pleasant fountain, bar, grocery store and 16th–17th-century Chiesa Santa Maria.

Standing in the piazza with the church behind you, walk straight ahead on Via di San Romano. At the quadruple fork in 500m turn partly right onto Via del Rossellino in the direction of Villa Gamberaia, which you reach in 800m after walking among olive groves. Just after the villa go under an ivy-covered archway and begin a moderately steep climb on the asphalt road between two tall stone walls.

At the top of the hill continue straight as the road becomes Via dei Crocifissalto. The road curves among olive groves and then ends at Via di Bagazzano. Turn left and immediately turn right onto Via di Terenzano, enjoying the beautiful views of the valley below. Continue past a house until the road appears to end at a T-junction with a cemetery up and to the left. Turn left and then turn right just before the cemetery. The path takes you down a hill, at first on cobblestones, and then past the Chiesa di San Martino di Terenzano. Turn left on the asphalt street and follow this road for the next 2.3km as it winds through olive orchards, then goes downhill past the railroad tracks where it finally ends at Strada Provinciale 110 in **Compiobbi** (11.1km).

Now turn right at the Strada Provinciale, cross under the railroad tracks and then cross the Via Arentina highway. ▶ Take the trail just past the newspaper kiosk at the right side of the piazza along the slow and lazy **Arno River**. In 300m turn left at a yellow utility tower and walk the steps up to the protected walk beside the highway. In 400m you come to the riverside town of **Ellera**. Continue as the walkway becomes a sidewalk and then briefly rejoin the highway at a traffic circle in the town of **Le Falle**.

Here in the small piazza are a bank, restaurant and café/bar.

Looking down toward Compiobbi

Just after the traffic circle look for a new, nondescript, yellow church on the left side of the road. Immediately after this turn left onto tiny Via Le Folle. Cross under the railroad tracks and cross the pedestrian bridge that spans the creek. Follow the walkway, then turn left at its end and follow Via Gricigliano uphill beside a yellow apartment building. At the fork in 300m turn right onto Via Paretaio.

The road veers to the right and in 700m crosses back under the railroad bridge. Turn left at the highway and follow it on the wide, left shoulder for 200m to the town of **Sieci** (14.2km). Walk on the highway's sidewalk and cross the Arno tributary on the highway bridge. Just after the bridge, turn right onto the pedestrian walkway along the river. Either turn left at 150m to find services in Sieci or continue along the path to enjoy a more peaceful walk among the picnic areas of the park until the path's end at Via Toscanini.

Turn left here and two blocks later go straight across the Via Arentina at the traffic circle. Cross under the railway bridge, pass Via Mandorli on the left and 200m later come to a wooden guardrail on the right. After the guardrail, branch right off the asphalt road onto a gravel road leading to a villa above. Before the villa, turn right onto another gravel road, toward a utility pole with a red/white CAI (Club Alpino Italiano) marker. Pass the pole and continue to the top of the hill.

Just after the house and barn at the top of the road, turn left and continue uphill. Turn right at the asphalt road in 200m and follow this road, continuing uphill as you enjoy sweeping panoramas of the surrounding vineyards and hills. Stay on the asphalt road and in 2km come to a branch leading left toward the church of **San Martin Quona**, which you have seen from a distance. Instead go straight ahead and in another 1km come to a triple fork with Via San Martin Quona on the left. Take the middle

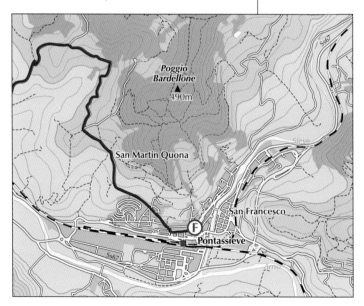

fork for the start of your final, long downhill among vine-yards and olive groves.

Before the road's end you pass through olive groves, go past two cemeteries and then finally come to homes on the outskirts of **Pontassieve**. At the end of the road turn left and in 400m come to the first gate, leading to the heart of town. Just after the gate is the Piazza Vittorio Emanuele II and the town's shops, café/bar, church and Municipio.

PONTASSIEVE 108M POP 20,622

In the Middle Ages, Pontassieve was called 'Castel Sant'Angelo' for the Florentine castle built here. The town later became known for its strategic bridge across the Sieve River, which opened to Florence the territories of Mugello and Casentino. By the 18th century Pontassieve's location made it a regional economic hub, and in the 19th and 20th centuries the railroad made it an industrial center. Its economic importance led the Allies to bomb the town repeatedly during World War II. Although none of its medieval features remain, the town was rebuilt along its medieval lines, with winding roads that follow the contours of the riverbank. The modern town hall is built on the foundations of the original medieval castle, and Via Ghiberti, the bustling, central commercial road, connects it with the Sieve bridge as in days past. Today, Pontassieve is a hub for artisanal leather, Chianti wine, olive oil, and handmade glass and pottery.

Most convenient for pilgrims is Toscani da Sempre (Via Fratelli Monzecchi 13/15, tel 558 392952, info@toscanidasempre.it, €50/70, breakfast available for pilgrims). In the lower town, by the river, is Albergo I Villini B&B (Viale Armando Diaz 28, tel 558 368140, info@ivillini.it, €52). Most economical is Leonardo's Rooms (Via Piave 7, tel 558 368192, info@leonardosrooms.it, €45/55).

STAGE 2

Pontassieve to Passo della Consuma

Start	Piazza Vittorio Emanuel II, Pontassieve
Finish	Main piazza, Consuma
Distance	17.8km
Total ascent	1021m
Total descent	138m
Difficulty	Moderate
Duration	6hrs
Note	The sole possibility for refreshment after Pontassieve is the bar at Diacceto, so it may be wise to bring provisions for the whole day.

A constant uphill track takes you from vineyards into the forests that will be your setting for the next five days. Today's climb is to the top of a saddle of mountains that separate two sections of the Arno River. Although about two-thirds of today's walk is on pavement, the often-spectacular views over vineyards and through forests to the green mountains of the Central Apennine range make this an enjoyable stage.

From Piazza Vittorio Emanuel II walk toward the Municipale and turn right onto Via Tanzini. Go under the clock tower arch and veer left as the road becomes Via Ghiberti. ▶ In 500m the road veers right and you cross the Sieve on a stout bridge. After the crossing continue along the road, passing the lovely **Chiesa San Francesco** on the right. One block later turn left on Via Bettini. At Via Farulla turn right and in one block come to the Via Forlivese, the main road up and down the Sieve Valley.

Just across the street is the barely visible **Via Tirolo**. Take it uphill, first crossing a railroad bridge. You will climb uphill on this pleasant, asphalt lane for the next 2.9km, with beautiful views of the Sieve Valley and the 10th-century **Castello di Nipozzano**, now a prosperous winery of the historic Frescobaldi company. The asphalt

Note the grocery store and bakery for provisions.

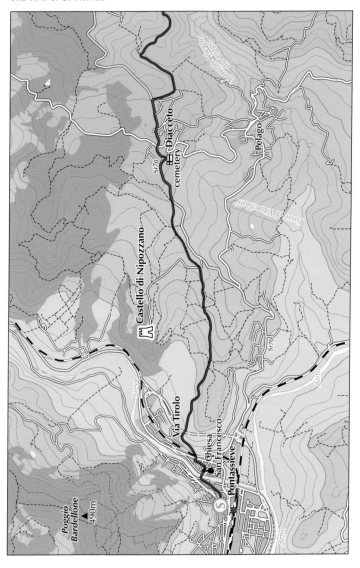

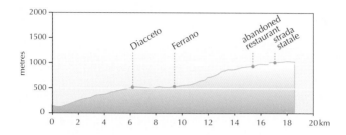

road ends among olive orchards near the top of the hill at an intersection marked 'Via di Castello Nipozzano.'

Cross the intersection onto the gravel road between two stone walls and continue uphill. In 800m cross an asphalt road and continue straight, enjoying the views of mountains and vineyards. Cross the highway in a couple hundred meters and continue uphill on the gravel vineyard road on the other side.

The view from the bridge over the Sieve River in Pontassieve

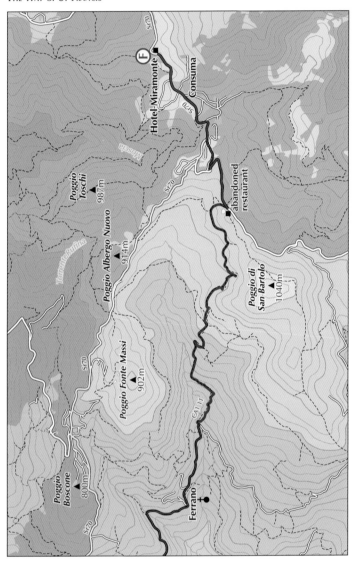

In 700m the vineyard road turns right toward a cemetery. Follow it 50m to the first wall of the **cemetery**, then turn left and follow the wall to the cemetery's driveway. Turn left here and continue 100m to the highway. At the highway turn right, going uphill into the village of **Diacceto** (6km). ▶

Continue uphill 400m on the highway to the turnoff for Ferrano. Turn right here to follow this forested, quiet and fairly level asphalt road for 4.3km until it turns to gravel. Soon, dramatic vistas of the forests and mountains around Pelago become visible, and a castle-like villa and the pointed, yellow tower of Chiesa San Pietro in **Ferrano** can be seen to the right.

Just past the church (9.1km) a little bench offers a place for a rest and snack. About 20mins after this the road turns to gravel and just afterward you come to an abandoned chapel on the right. Here you cross a bridge and just afterward on the left is the trailhead for the forested path to Consuma, signed 'Consuma 1.45.' Turn left and follow the gravel path, **CAI 11**, uphill, looking continually for the red/white painted waymarks of the official trail.

In 700m is an important and unmarked fork: two broad paths branch off, one toward the right among fir trees, the

The bar on the left side at the turnoff for Pelago is the last place for services until the end of the day's walk.

San Pietro is visible for several kilometres along the forested mountainside

57

other to the left among deciduous trees. Turn left, and in 20m see a red/white CAI marker that confirms you're going the right way. Soon the path starts uphill and in 700m a CAI 11 marker tells you to turn left at a T-junction.

In just 500m you come to a meadow that is bisected by a two-track gravel road. There are no markings here, but turn left on the gravel road. The road goes uphill and in 50m turns to concrete. In 200m at a triple fork, turn right at another unmarked intersection. In just 20m you seen a CAI marker on a dead fir tree to the right. In 300m you come to another intersection, this time marked with ample signs. Go left and uphill, continuing to follow CAI 11.

The path now changes to concrete and 300m later comes to a forest road. Turn left. In 1.4km you come to a green chain link fence on the right and soon afterwards a road, Via La Catena. Turn left and follow this road for 700m to an intersection where you take CAI SM (Sentiero della Memoria) right, toward Consuma. This quiet road goes uphill and curves to the right and then in 400m comes to an asphalt road and the **abandoned restaurant** Il Laghetto Nil Bosco. Turn left onto the asphalt road at the direction of the signs for CAI 6.

Follow the asphalt road for 900m until, after a left bend in the road, the CAI markings point you onto a small trail on the right side that offers a shortcut into Consuma. Turn right and go uphill. Follow the road at the top to the right, through scattered vacation homes to La Baita Ristorante. Just afterward turn right onto the **SR70 highway** and follow its left shoulder for about 800m into the heart of **Consuma** with its restaurants and shops. The main piazza is on the right side of the road across from the village church.

CONSUMA 1050M POP 150

The hamlet of Consuma sits on the Florence side of Passo della Consuma, the main crossing over a spine of the Central Appennines that separates two parts of the Arno River drainage. The town traces its roots to the 15th century when it is first noted as a village that served travelers between Arezzo and Florence. It now serves vacationers visiting the Casentino National Park on two-lane SR70. A central feature of the settlement is its church, built in 1932 over the foundations of a 16th-century chapel.

Marcello Carletti and his daughter, Irina, have eight rooms with 17 beds available for pilgrims at Panificio e Pizzeria in the heart of Consuma (Via Casentinese 331, tel 0558 306440, irina.consuma@yahoo.it, €30/50 includes breakfast). The other lodging is the threadbare but friendly Hotel Miramonti (tel 0558 306566, info@hotelmiramonti-ar.it, breakfast available), 1km beyond the town, just past the top of the pass and 200m from tomorrow's track.

STAGE 3
Consuma to Stia

Start	Piazza, Consuma
Finish	Fattoria La Foresta, Stia
Distance	17km
Total ascent	536m
Total descent	1093m
Difficulty	Hard
Duration	6hrs 15mins
Note	No services are available along the way, so plan to purchase provisions the night before.

A couple of very steep climbs make this a difficult walk, but otherwise this is a long, downhill hike on forested mountain paths and quiet farm roads. Leave early to enjoy the delightful town of Stia on the banks of the Arno.

▶ From the piazza head uphill 800m to the top of the pass. Across from the log house bar at the summit find the **trailhead** marked 'So.F.T. Trekking, Anello Principale.' Take this trail as it leads gently uphill and away from the highway under beech and pine trees.

If you stayed at the Hotel Miramonte, return 200 meters to the top of the pass to rejoin the route.

59

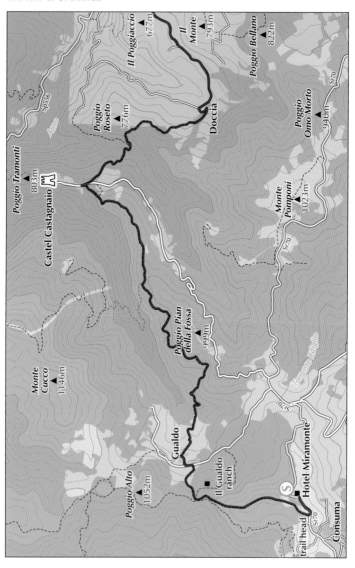

In 400m you come to an intersection with a gravel road heading downhill toward **Il Gualdo horse ranch**. At this confusing intersection follow a path marked 'Stia 00' just to the left of the Il Gualdo road. You come to a fence and follow it toward a group of houses and finally an asphalt road where you turn left.

Shortly afterward go right at the road sign for Gualdo (3km), following the plentiful CAI '00CT' markers downhill on the asphalt road through the tiny town toward a

The sign for the easy-to-miss path above Il Gualdo horse ranch

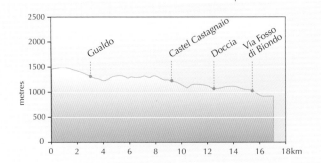

house marked '25,' where the road comes to a T-junction. Continuing to follow the CAI markers, in 425m you arrive at the two-track driveway of a two-story house with a green metal fence. Walk clockwise around the fence and then take an overgrown path at the corner of the house, leading downhill.

Cross another creek on stones at the bottom of the narrow path. After crossing the creek stay on the right side and then ascend steeply for the next 500m. After the climb, the path widens and another ascent begins. Continue on this path without deviating for another 450m.

Now the path starts to descend steeply over loose stones, branches and bedrock. Pass a small stone building with a red tile roof on the right and continue to follow the red/white CAI '00' markers uphill along a wide, earthen path under beech and pine trees to the top of a rise. Continue on and soon see views open up to the left.

Follow the CAI markers on this pathway and continue uphill, avoiding forks to the left and right. You finally reach the summit and begin a descent for 700m, at first gradual and then steep. Pass a pump house operated by a solar cell, continue downhill and in 400m come to the asphalt road leading to the settlement of **Castel Castagnaio** (10.5km). At the pavement turn right.

In a couple of hundred meters take a **path** to the left marked 'Stia Sentiero 72.' This wide path descends for the next several hundred meters. In 500m come to an intersection and continue straight ahead onto this grassy path. After a creek crossing on stones it is tempting to take the wide gravel road to the left, but instead go uphill, finding an overgrown path next to the CAI marker, to the right of the gravel road. Take this path and climb steeply uphill.

In 600m the path begins to widen out and descend. Come to a dry creek and in a couple hundred meters this path is joined by a wider path, which you follow to the left. Soon a pasture appears. Follow the road down past a vegetable garden and fountain into tiny **Doccia** (11.7km), a scattered settlement of farmhouses and outbuildings.

Walk past a house marked '24' and go right, following the gravel drive among more houses. Stay on this gravel

The view downward toward Doccia

road for the next 3.5km, enjoying sweeping vistas to the left of mountains, farms and **Castello Porciano**. ▶ Avoid all driveways to the left and right, until you come to Via Fosso

Note the kiosks at various intervals that describe the history and culture of the area.

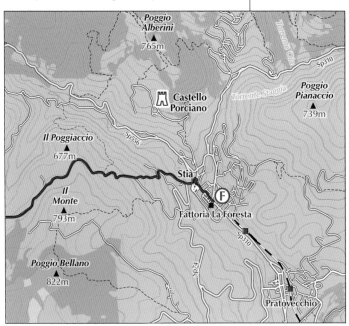

The Church of Santa Maria Asunta in Stia's main piazza

di Biondo (15.2km) on the left. Take this road downhill.
Stia becomes visible below as the road turns to the left. At
a junction of four roads take the lower road to the right,
continuing the descent into Stia.

Soon the sounds of the Arno River below are audible
and you come to a commercial road on the outskirts of
Stia. Turn left toward the old center of Stia and cross the
bridge. After crossing the bridge turn left and go uphill
briefly, then turn right just after the church on the Via San
Francesco. The lane quickly arrives in the heart of Stia's
Centro Storico with Chiesa Santa Maria Assunta, as well
as restaurants, shops, bars and hotel Albergo Falterona.

For Fattoria La Foresta continue downhill at this pedestrian mall and follow the sounds of a waterfall down and
to the left. Cross in front of the waterfall, keeping it on the
left, and go uphill along the shops and stores of the Via
Roma toward a gas station sign. Pass a piazza on the left,
cross a street, and the **Fattoria La Foresta** is on the left.

STIA 441M POP 2990

Stia and its sister city, Pratovecchio (pop 2075, elev 420m), immediately to
the south, combine to serve as the economic hub of the Upper Arno Valley.
Originally the market town for the Porciano Castle to the northwest, Stia became
a textile manufacturing center during the Industrial Revolution. In 1838 its largest wool mill employed over 500 people and produced 700,000 meters of cloth.
Today it is a recreational hub and resort town, serving visitors to the Casentino
national park. At the heart of its central piazza is the Church of Santa Maria
Assunta. Although the church's facade is from the 19th century, stone columns in
the dark and peaceful nave are decorated with plants, animals and human figures
in the Romanesque and Early Gothic styles of six or seven centuries earlier. A
terra cotta Madonna and child are examples of the work of Andrea della Robbia
(born 1435), seen throughout the region.

The elegant Albergo Falterona (Piazza Bernado Tanucci 85, tel 0575 504569,
info@albergofalterona.it, €55/75) is open seasonally, as is the economical
Fattoria La Foresta (Via Roma 2 7, tel 0575 582032, laforestahotel@gmail.com,
April to October, €45/70, breakfast included). The Domus Pacis hostel of Santa
Maria Asunta church has 22 beds available for pilgrims (tel 0575 583722, info@
parrocchiastia.com, €25).

STAGE 4
Stia to Camaldoli (village)

Start	Fattoria La Foresta, Stia
Finish	Monastero di Camaldoli
Distance	16.6km
Total ascent	1017m
Total descent	583m
Difficulty	Hard
Duration	6hrs
Note	After leaving Stia there are no services until arriving at Eremo Camaldoli, so bring plenty of food and water.

Today's walk climbs CAI trails 72, 76 and 70 up into the mountains of the Foreste Casentinesi national park, offering wide panoramas of its thickly wooded peaks. With good timing a visit is possible to Eremo Camaldoli, an important Benedictine monastery of deep and genuine calm that has been tucked into this high valley since the 11th century. After a steep downhill to the tiny village of Camaldoli, you will have earned a good rest.

Starting at Fattoria La Foresta, go toward central Stia and immediately turn right on Via Veneto, walking uphill. Pass the elementary school on the right and in about 400m

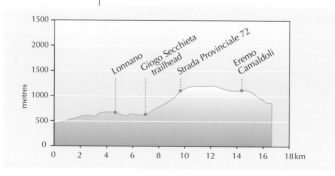

come to some steps at a sign reading Planetario del Parco Nazionale. ▶ Climb the steps and, steering toward the left of the **planetario**, find the asphalt road again.

Turn right on the road and go uphill. Climb another set of steps and arrive at a children's play area; go through the play area and around the yellow apartment building on the left side, continuing to follow the road uphill. Cross a street and continue uphill to a modern chapel. Turn left here on the unmarked Viale 17 Partigiani. Still following the CAI markers, turn right at the next intersection.

Soon the markers lead to a path on the left that goes steeply uphill, the first of several that offer shortcuts as the road makes its own, lazier climb on switchbacks. In 100m come to a small shrine – **Madonna del Poggio**. Turn left here, noting the sign that reads 'Eremo di Camaldoli 5.0 hours,' and just afterward follow a fence with vineyards on the opposite side. In 200m you are back on the road, where you turn left. In a further 200m the road turns to gravel and goes downhill toward a seasonal creek. ▶

Continue along the road for 650m; it crosses an asphalt road and then continues for 150m at which point

Note the CAI markers for 72, which is the path for most of the way.

In 2014 the road washed out about 100m from here and was impassible for cars but suitable for pedestrians.

The shrine to Madonna del Poggio (Madonna of the Mountain) outside Stia

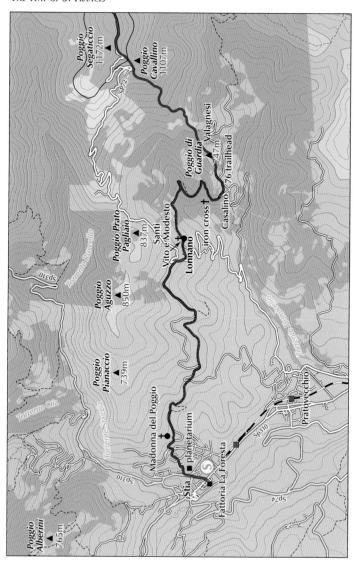

it comes to the same asphalt road again. This time turn right, with wide views back to Stia and beyond.

At the first curve of the road is a driveway to the right and just afterwards, the path. Turn right onto the path, going uphill. Follow the path for about 1km as it goes downhill then steeply uphill before meeting the Strada Vicinale della Madonnina asphalt road. Turn right, following the waymarks and enjoying the beautiful vistas of Stia behind you.

In 1km the road comes to an intersection where you turn right toward the town of Lonnano. Just 150m later, at a Y intersection, turn left, and in another 100m come to the upper part of **Lonnano** and the charming 10th–12th-century Chiesa dei Santi Vito e Modesto a Lonnano. Pass the church to the left and walk downhill just after the parking area. Soon there is a triple-fork intersection where you go straight ahead toward three tall pine trees, the last bearing a CAI mark.

Take a fork going right in 200m, after which is a fountain. Just afterward, turn right at another fork and walk downhill in the direction of a barn and farmhouse, which you pass alongside. In 200m the path turns right at a gate and follows the fence line steeply downhill on gravel. The narrow path gently undulates up and down, crossing a creek after 150m.

In 700m pass by a house and in another 200m come to a road. Turn right, following the markings, and in 400m come to a two-track gravel road. Turn left, noting the **iron cross** marked '1908.' Immediately turn left again, going uphill, and in just a few meters don't miss the right turn at a fork in the path.

In 100m come to an asphalt road making a U curve. A sign shows that Casalino is to the right. Turn left, going uphill, and looking back you can see Stia again, receding into the distance in the valley below. Pass a monastery of Franciscan nuns to the right and in 400m, after a curve, turn left off the asphalt road at a grouping of signs. Note in particular one that reads 'Giogo Secchieta **76**' – this is the trail for the next 3.3km.

Here there are spectacular views both north and south.

The trail goes steeply upward and is punctuated in 400m by a clearing at a ridge between two mountain peaks. ◄ Continue uphill at the clearing, always watching for the red/white CAI markings, noting signs for Giogo Secchieta. Along the way is an intersection with a gravel road and twice a tempting diversion onto a paved road on the left.

A third time the path rises up to meet the road, which is the very quiet **Strada Provinciale 72**. This time go onto the pavement and turn right. You will stay on this road for the next 4.4km as it winds its way gently through fairytale forests of mature birch trees, then among tall pine trees. Several paths branch off, but stay on this road until you reach the turn marked 'Camaldoli 7, Eremo Camaldoli.' Turn left and in just 300m arrive at the front gates of the **Eremo Camaldoli**.

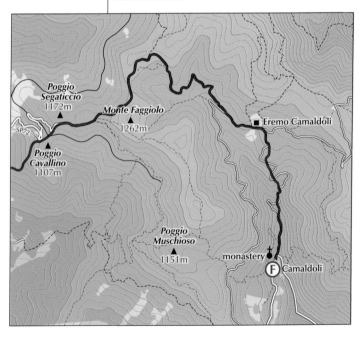

MONASTIC COMMUNITY OF CAMALDOLI

Behind an iron fence lie the individual hermitages at Camaldoli

Nestled in an ancient forest high above Stia, the Camaldoli community is famous in monastic circles for following a rigorous interpretation of the monastic Rule of St Benedict. The community has produced an illustrious array of church leaders since its establishment in the 11th century – four cardinals, countless bishops and many artists, including Guido d'Arezzo, the inventor of modern musical notation.

Established by St Romuald in about 1023, the site was a field (*campus* in Latin) donated by a patron, Maldolus – hence 'Campus Maldolus' or Camaldoli. The local community encompasses the upper Hermitage (Eremo) of Camaldoli and the lower Monastery of Camaldoli, set 4km below in the tiny Camaldoli village. The order includes another 14 hermitages and monasteries in Italy, Poland, Brazil and the US.

Camaldoli's separate facilities for hermit monks and communal monks demonstrate the dual influences within Camaldolism – solitary asceticism as well as communal monastic life. The hermitage is divided between semi-public spaces that include a guest hall and chapel, and 20 individual hermitages sequestered behind a locked fence. In the village, the monastic community includes a public chapel and guesthouse. Both facilities offer pharmacy stores that sell artisanal herbal products. The buildings date from the 16th–18th centuries.

The monastery is open for visits throughout the day, while the hermitage is closed except during specified visiting hours that change with the season. (www.monasterodicamaldoli.it; Hermitage: eremo@camaldoli.it, tel 0575 556021; Monastery: monastero@camaldoli.it, tel 0575 556012.)

After your visit to the *emero*, pass the Antica Farmacia, Libreria and Caffe and follow the road downhill. This lane is labeled CAI 70 and Cammino San Vicino, and you will see on the downhill side several opportunities to shorten the trip by taking the steep paths that connect the asphalt loops.

In 1.8km, at the bottom of the hill, turn left, cross a stone bridge and pass a small stone chapel. In 200m you arrive at the post office and tourist information office of **Camaldoli village**. Directly ahead is Monastero Camaldoli and slightly farther are the two hotels and the restaurants and shops of quiet Camaldoli village.

CAMALDOLI VILLAGE 874M POP 35

With advance registration by email or phone it is possible to stay at the La Foresteria guesthouse of the Monastero Camaldoli (tel 0575 556013, foresteria@camaldoli.it), which has 154 beds in simple rooms and a large dining hall that seats 250. Just a few meters away are Locanda dei Baroni (tel 0575 556015, locanda@itrebaroni.it, from €55 with half board available) with its adjacent restaurant, and Albergo Ristorante Camaldoli (tel 0575 556019, from €50, including breakfast) with its bakery, restaurant and tobacco store.

STAGE 5
Camaldoli to Badia Prataglia

Start	Monastero di Camaldoli
Finish	Parish church, Badia Prataglia
Distance	8.4km
Total ascent	534m
Total descent	519m
Difficulty	Moderate
Duration	3hrs 30mins
Note	There are no services available on the trail, but a few snacks and some water for this short day should be sufficient.

After an hour's steep climb this short stage becomes a very agreeable and restful walk along the CAI 072 trail to the pleasant resort town of Badia Prataglia. The short distance allows a rest for tomorrow's more difficult walk to Santuario della Verna.

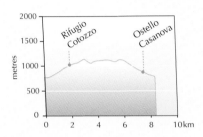

From the front door of the monastery turn right, walk downhill, round the corner on the main road and cross the stone bridge. Look immediately to the left for a trail-head with several markers. Go uphill here toward Rifugio Cotozzo.

The climb is steep for the first 100m then levels out for a bit. In another 400m come to an intersection and follow the signs to the left. In another 400m turn left, always following the red/white striped markers of CAI 072.

Cross a creek and 600m later come to **Rifugio Cotozzo**, a stone shelter with a simple table, fireplace and bench inside. Follow the sign that points uphill.

Near the top of the climb follow the sign that points right to Badia Prataglia. In just 100m is the first of two summits of today's climb.

Just afterward there is a tempting left turn going uphill, but stay on CAI 072. In 400m come to a creek as the trail turns toward the right. It is easy to lose the trail here so look carefully for red/white markings. After a meadow of ferns continue uphill, coming to another high

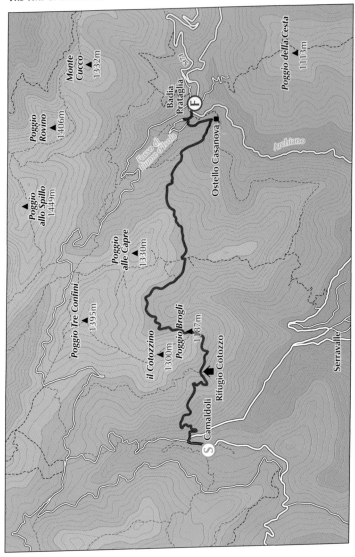

point in 350m. After a short descent the trail becomes fairly level and wide, through a pleasant beech forest. In 300m cross a creek on stones.

The simple and bare Rifugio Cotozzo

In 600m, at an intersection, take a left toward a forest clearing. The climb begins again and in 400m is an important intersection. Facing the sign, go left. Now we see two options – a wide path that goes uphill on the left or an obscure path to its right. Go right and follow the path into a forest clearing where the red/white markings begin to appear again.

Come to a creek and make a left turn, following markers on the left side. Afterward, at another fern-covered forest clearing, look to the right for the red/white markings. Forested vistas now appear on the right and soon the descent begins through a beautiful beech forest.

In 500m the descent becomes steep. In another 300m come to a fork in the road and turn right, again following the red/white markers. In 400m the path turns right and is joined by another path from the left. Continue downhill, descending through a forest of oak and pine. Come to a green gate and in 100m see a white chalet-style building

*View from the
trail down to
Badia Prataglia*

with green shutters. This is **Ostello Casanova Casentino** (8km). You are close to the end of the day and may want to consider an overnight here.

Turn into the parking lot and, keeping the hostel on the right, pass the brown gate. Here a wide path leads downhill on a shortcut into Badia Prataglia, with peek-a-boo views toward the red roofs of the resort village on the right side.

In a few hundred meters come to a house with a stone-and-wood fence atop a stone wall. Pass it on the right and arrive at an asphalt road, the Via Vetriceta Bassa. Turn right and follow the road downhill to another asphalt road, the Via Vetriceta. Turn right again and come shortly to the main street of **Badia Prataglia**.

At the intersection see two overnight options: Pensione La Foresta on the right and Pensione Giardino on the left. Ahead is the parish church and to the right is the tourist information office. Just to the left of the parish church is one of several grocery stores with provisions available for tomorrow's strenuous climb to Santuario della Verna.

BADIA PRATAGLIA 835M POP 901

The resort town of Badia Prataglia traces its roots back to the early 11th century with the establishment of its monastery, of which the town's parish church, dedicated to Santa Asunta and St Bartholomew, is the last remaining evidence. Although the exterior of the church appears modern, 20th-century remodeling revealed architectural features from its 11th- and 12th-century roots, particularly its crypt which was discovered and restored in 1910.

Plentiful supplies of excellent birch, chestnut and oak from the surrounding forests, coupled with long winter nights spent in relative isolation, have created the right environment for the local woodworking craft to flourish. Badia Prataglia is filled with vacation homes and hotels that serve part-time residents and visitors who want to enjoy the beauty of the Casentino National Forest.

Right on the path 700m above town is Ostello Casanova Casentino (tel 0575 559897, Casanova@rifugionelcasentino.it, from €35, includes breakfast). While mostly for groups it is the town's most economical option. The modern Pensione La Foresta (Via Nazionale 13, tel 0575 559009, info@albergolaforesta.eu, €45) is in the heart of town, just across the street from the larger Pensione Giardino (Via Nazionale 15, tel 0575 559016, hotelgiardino@virgilio.it, €55).

STAGE 6
*Badia Prataglia to
Santuario della Verna*

Start	Parish church of Badia Prataglia
Finish	Santuario della Verna
Distance	17.5km
Total ascent	1194m
Total descent	959m
Difficulty	Hard
Duration	7hrs 30mins
Note	Shopping for the day's food the night before in the plentiful shops of Badia Prataglia is a better option than depending on the tiny restaurant at Rimbocchi, which may be closed at lunchtime.

This challenging day follows the CAI trails 073, 070 and 053, as well as the Senteiro delle Foreste Sacre, through lush forests with sweeping vistas of the surrounding mountains and valleys. There are some serious climbs both up and down as you make your way to the village of Frassineta (no services) and Rimbocchi (bar/café) in advance of your final, steep climb to St Francis' beloved and beautiful La Verna. The end result is well worth the effort, as the essence of St Francis still permeates this holy mountain retreat.

Facing the parish church, go left between the church and the grocery store on Via Eden, also marked CAI 073AR. Passing the grocery store and church, walk down the asphalt road rather than up onto the highway to leave the village. At 500m take a fork to the left onto the quiet lane Via La Casa where the homes become sparser and a descent begins.

At the bottom of the hill cross the river on the bridge with a metal railing. The road now becomes gravel, with a hayfield on the left, and soon begins to climb. In 200m come to a fork and turn left, then immediately at the next fork turn right. In 50m go through the gate and make certain it is closed behind you. Continue on the path through the forest and a few minutes later come to a path on the left. Turn left and uphill, following the CAI markings along the way.

Now the path starts to ascend steeply on bedrock and loose gravel, soon becoming a narrow earthen track that leads up through the trees. In 200m the path begins

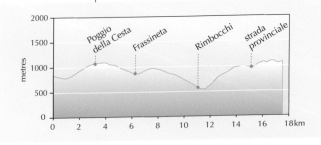

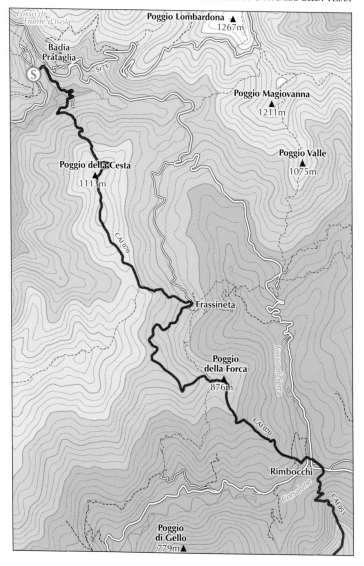

to level out a bit and in another 300m is a fern meadow. Watch your footing here and carefully look for the CAI markings toward the right to guide you.

Soon after the meadow is a creek, which you cross and then continue walking up and to the right. The path now climbs steeply into a beech forest. In 400m you come to a second fern meadow. Again, veer toward the right, searching out the CAI markings. At 150m past the fern meadow turn left and cross a seasonal creek bed where the path begins to level out.

Turn right here at the intersecting trail in 150m, and in another 300m come to the summit of **Poggio della Cesta** (1113m) at a clearing with power lines and a concrete utility post. Go straight, begin a descent into a forest of oak trees, and soon after start climbing again.

In 800m is the last of three small summits, after which you begin a long and pleasant descent on the arm of a ridge through oak forests, with wide vistas to the right. In a further 800m you arrive at a green government gate; go through this and in 150m come to a second, similar gate. After passing the gate continue downhill. In another 200m is a series of trail signs: follow the signs toward Frassineta. The path becomes wide and goes steeply downhill, and after about 1km you arrive first at a small chapel, then at a church below and to the right in **Frassineta** (6.1km). ◄

The lawn in front of the church makes a pleasant rest stop.

After passing the church, stay on CAI 070, which at this point is an asphalt road on the uphill side of town. Shortly the asphalt turns to a two-track gravel road, which then begins to ascend and 800m later arrives at another green gate. Pass the gate on the left and continue.

Soon you reach a wooden gate. Go through it and close it behind you, and 40m later turn left and walk along the fence. In 100m the path leads into the forest again and after the fence a gradual descent begins. Wide views of the surrounding countryside appear on the right side.

Turn left on the trail marked as CAI 070 and continue downhill. In 250m you see a sign showing you are

Halfway between Frassineta and Rimbocchi

halfway between Frassineta and Rimbocchi. In just 50m turn left at the sign for Rimbocchi, where you begin a climb, and in 100m come to the summit of **Poggio della Forca** (876m).

Continue heading along the ridge, with sparse oak trees and vistas to the right and left as a steep descent begins. Some 600m later there is a large, abandoned microwave reflector on the right. Soon after passing this odd relic is a meadow with 180-degree views of the surrounding mountains and valleys.

Continue carefully down the hill on the eroded and sometimes slippery path. In 300m the path becomes a gravel road and begins to flatten out. At the next intersection go straight and note the sign that says 'Rimbocchi: .3 hrs.' As you continue downhill you are rewarded with constant views ahead and to the left and right.

Soon turn left at another path crossing and 100m later come to a small clearing. Continue to the left,

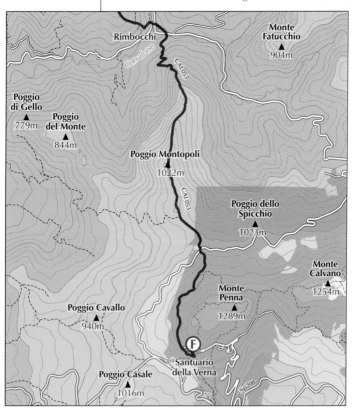

joining a small road. Just after the clearing is another intersection: turn left here and in 100m turn right. Follow the power lines as they guide you downhill toward the town of Rimbocchi, which you can now see below.

A hand-lettered sign offers the option of continuing to follow the power lines down a steep bank or turning left along the road. The steep option is slightly slippery in a few places, but otherwise passable. Follow this trail down and then, at a hairpin turn, go right. Soon the village of **Rimbocchi** (11.2km) appears. ▶

Here the route changes to CAI 053, which you follow the rest of the day. Go left, along the main street of the village, and come to a fountain with potable water on the right. At the junction of the main street and the highway look for the CAI 053 marker that says 'La Verna: 2.55 hours.' Cross the highway and go downhill on the path toward the creek. Cross the creek on stones and begin climbing on CAI 053. (Over the next several kilometers the path will ascend about 600m.)

The climb becomes very strenuous in 300m, but you are rewarded with majestic views. After a time you arrive at the summit of **Poggio Montopoli** (1022m). Continue straight and in 700m come to an intersection with CAI 052. Go left, continuing on 053. In 100m CAI 054 turns off to the left; continue straight and 50m later see a pond on the right. Just afterward is the **Strada Provinciale** Alto Corsalone (15.3km). Cross the road and get back on the trail, noting the sign that says, 'La Verna: .50 hrs.'

After the road is a fairytale forest, with boulders covered in green moss and sunlight filtered through layers of birch leaves. In 150m come to an intersection and turn right, remaining on 053, now also called Anello Basso (lower ring). ▶ Watch carefully for CAI markers as you weave through the gentle and cool forest.

Soon you come to a giant rock looming on the left, and after that a clearing where you see that the rock is part of the mountain that forms the foundation of the convent buildings above. Follow the trail up and around a gate and then continue on the trail as it circles to the front entry and reception desk of **Santuario della Verna**.

At a small park there are picnic tables and kiosks with maps, and across the quiet highway is a bar/café, which may be open.

Note the many cataracts in the large boulders – perhaps St Francis or his friends used these for prayer and meditation.

SANTUARIO DELLA VERNA 1160M

Santuario della Verna is widely considered one of the most holy and spiritual places in all of Italy. Among the ancient trees and rocky crags on the south side of Mt Penna (1128m) it is easy to imagine St Francis in deep meditation or quiet prayer. La Verna's remote location has allowed it to retain much of the same character as when St Francis walked its paths 800 years ago.

On 8 May 1213, out of his love and admiration for the holy man, Count Orlando of Chiusi spontaneously made Francis a gift of the site, writing that the gift was, 'for the health of my soul.' Francis loved the mountain, especially the craggy rocks with hidden chambers where he could pray and meditate, and he came here often.

It was here, in the autumn of 1214, that Francis discovered sharp, nail-like protrusions on his hands and an open wound on his side. He shared the existence of these 'stigmata' with only his closest friends. At the examination of his body at his death at Santa Maria degli Angeli in Assisi in 1226, more than a dozen sworn witnesses confirmed the presence of these marks of the crucifixion.

A self-guided tour of the convent complex begins at the central piazzale with the 14th–15th-century Basilica, which houses relics of St Francis and features white terra cotta bas-relief sculptures by the 15th-century sculptor Andrea della Robbia. The bones of Count Orlando are interred in the adjacent 13th-century Church of Santa Maria degli Angeli, which is accessed from the sacristy of the basilica.

Returning to the piazzale from the Basilica, continue along the ambulatory and its series of large murals depicting the life of Francis, then linger in the diverse chapels leading at the far end to the 13th-century Chapel of the Stigmata, which includes another terra cotta by Robbia, this one of the Crucifixion. Along the way is a small cave remembered as the bed of St Francis, where a person can spend a few moments in a place that most certainly was once graced by the humble man of Assisi.

Twice daily the friars walk in procession from the Santa Maria church to the Chapel of the Stigmata, and on 17 September of each year pilgrims from neighboring parishes come to La Verna to worship, remember and celebrate Italy's patron saint.

The sanctuary has a pilgrim hostel, La Foresteria, with 72 renovated hotel-style rooms (tel 0575 534210, santuarioverna@gmail.com, €57 includes breakfast and a large group dinner). A limited number of pilgrim beds are available in the convent's dormitory, with maximum one overnight and dinner by donation (tel 0575 5341, amministrazione@santuariolaverna.org). In Chiusi della Verna, located 1.5km below the convent, two small hotels also offer accommodation. Hotel Ristorante Bellavista (Viale San Francesco 17, tel 0575 599029, gilberto.gabelli@gmail.com, €45/65 includes breakfast) and Albergo Letizia (Via Roma 26, tel 0575 599020, info@albergo-letizia.it, €40/55 includes breakfast). Note that the gates of the convent close at 10.00pm and the hostel doors are locked at 10.30pm.

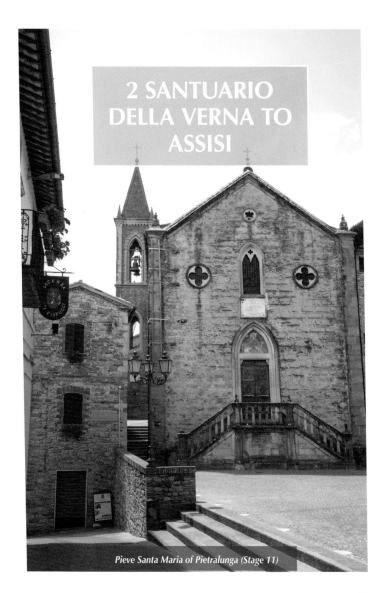

2 SANTUARIO DELLA VERNA TO ASSISI

Pieve Santa Maria of Pietralunga (Stage 11)

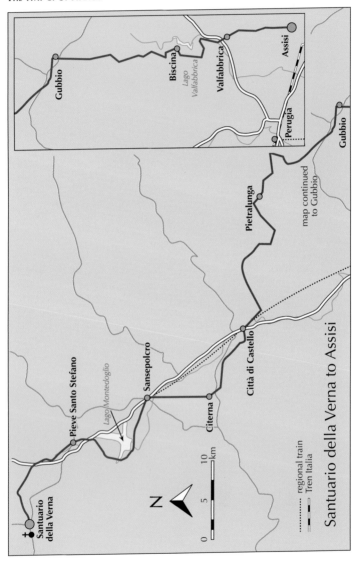

Gubbio

Biscina

Lago Valfabbrica

Valfabbrica

Assisi

Perugia

Gubbio

map continued to Gubbio

Pietralunga

Città di Castello

Citerna

Sansepolcro

Lago Montedoglio

Pieve Santo Stefano

Santuario della Verna

N

0   5   10 km

.... regional train
═══ Tren Italia

Santuario della Verna to Assisi

After passing over Mount Penna at Santuario della Verna, this 181km stretch of the Way of St Francis enters the valley of the Tiber River, which skirts Assisi and then flows through Rome on its way to the Tyrrhenian Sea at Ostia. The rich soil of this valley has made it an agricultural center for the Italian peninsula for many centuries. Pilgrims pass through farms of wheat, barley, rye and sunflowers in the lowlands. On the hillsides, vineyards give way to olive groves and pastures and then are replaced by forests of beech, oak and pine on the higher slopes of the rugged Central Apennine range.

The route leaves the main Tiber Valley at Città di Castello as industry and civilization make it less suitable for walking pilgrims. Instead, after Pietralunga the Chiascio River – a tributary of the Tiber – accompanies pilgrims to Assisi.

These river valleys and the surrounding mountains north of Assisi were much loved by Francis, and contain numerous legends of his encounters. The many churches and shrines remind residents and pilgrims of each place's particular experience of the saint. Most well known after his birthplace at Assisi is Gubbio, where Francis encountered the notorious wolf and where today tourists and pilgrims roam the picturesque medieval streets.

On the third stage of this part – partway between historic Sansepolcro and Citerna – pilgrims leave Tuscany behind and enter Umbria, a region known for its scenic beauty, delicious cuisine and close connection to St Francis.

Umbria is the heart of Franciscan pilgrimage country. Walking itineraries from Santuario della Verna and Gubbio to Assisi are popular among Italian pilgrims, so infrastructure becomes more plentiful. The reason is clear: Assisi beckons pilgrims to find inside its walls the treasured memories of Italy's patron saint.

Looking down on Bar Sasso and the Tiber Valley beyond (Stage 11)

STAGE 7

Santuario della Verna to Pieve Santo Stefano

Start	Portineria of Santuario della Verna
Finish	Piazza Santo Stefano, Pieve Santo Stefano
Distance	15.2km
Total ascent	309m
Total descent	983m
Difficulty	Easy
Duration	5hrs
Note	There are no services along the way, so plan to bring enough food and water from La Verna to make it to lunch.

Forests, mountains and trees are constant companions on this mostly downhill walk to the town of Pieve Santo Stefano, tucked into a narrow valley of the Tiber River. The trail markings are excellent, so it is easy to find the way on Sentiero Frasssati and CAI trails 50, 66 and 75. After two uphill stretches the remainder is a long descent.

Starting at the Portineria of Santuario della Verna, head down the flagstone path, through the gate and past the Statue of St Francis and the Dove Seller. Continue downhill, passing the lower parking lot and 100m later the tiny

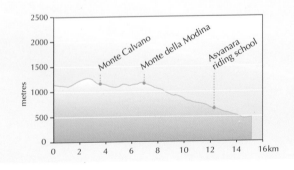

Statue of St Francis and the dove seller just outside La Verna's gates

Ristorante Piadina. In another 100m, at a sharp curve in the road, a trailhead appears on the left. Among the many markings is Sentiero Frassati, the day's first path. Turn left here, onto the gravel road.

In a couple hundred meters turn left onto a gravel path going uphill, again marked Sentiero Frassati. In 400m you arrive at a summit with a tall, wooden cross and a triple fork in the road. Go to the right on the CAI 050 trail – part of the Grande Escursione Appenninica (GEA), one of Italy's best-loved mountain trail networks. The trail now goes uphill steeply for 800m on a narrower

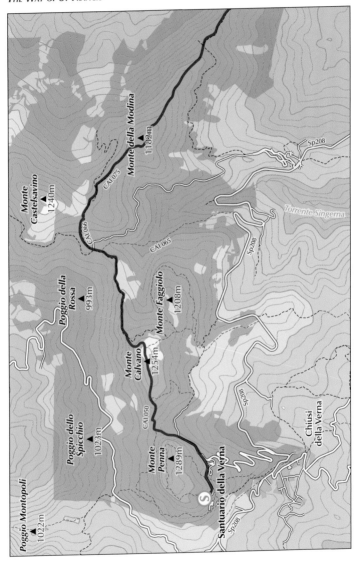

Poggio Montopoli
1022m

Poggio dello Spicchio
1023m

Poggio della Rossa
993m

Monte Castelsavino
1240m

Monte della Modina
1182m

Monte Faggiolo
1208m

Monte Calvano
1254m

Monte Penna
1289m

Santuario della Verna

Chiusi della Verna

Torrente Singerna

CAI 075

CAI 066

CAI 065

CAI 050

Sp208

Sp208

Sp208

path with beautiful views on the right side as it makes its way to **Monte Calvano** (1254m) (3.85km).

Just 75m later come to a barbed wire fence with a gate. Close the gate after you pass and come to a large, grassy meadow. Go through the meadow, veering toward the left and come to a cross, set at a cairn on the brow of the hill marked CAI 050/GEA. Pass the cross and continue down the meadow. On the right side in 200m is a way-mark pointing to the left for CAI 050. Go left, continuing to the end of the meadow where a small path begins, heading downhill.

In about 300m a gravel road from the right joins the trail. Continue left, and in short order pass through three

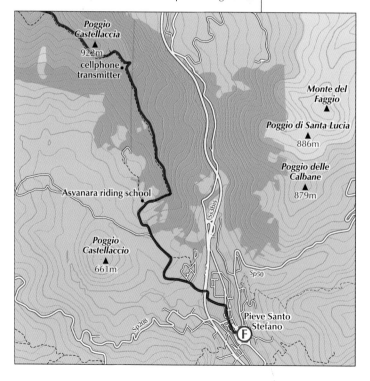

pasture gates of barbed wire. As always, close the gates behind you. After the third gate, CAI 065 branches to the right. Instead of turning right, stay on this path and in 100m come to an intersection with a gravel road. Go straight ahead onto CAI 066. Here the path begins going uphill. In 1km turn right at the fork, following CAI 075, soon reaching the summit of **Monte della Modina** (1181m) (6.9km).

After this, the long downhill stretch begins. You come to a section of charred trees in 800m, and in another 1km go straight at an intersection with a gravel road. Here you see a sign that says 18% grade. Continue on this road for 1.4km as it passes a **cell phone tower**.

In another 2km the road is joined by a driveway on the left and makes a sharp right turn. ◀ In 400m is the **Asvanara Riding School**, and in 200m the road turns to asphalt and continues downhill. At an intersection in 400m the road is joined by another road from the right, and two others from the left join 60m later. Go right and downhill. From here Pieve Santo Stefano is clearly visible below, less than 1km ahead.

In 200m pass the Punto Ristoro del Corso Francescano rest stop and just afterward cross the **SS3bis freeway** on an overpass. At a stop sign in 400m turn right on the Strada Provinciale 208, which you follow into town. Just after the tall stone church turn left, go one block and turn left again onto the Piazza Santo Stefano, the heart of **Pieve Santo Stefano**.

From here you can look down and see Pieve Santo Stefano tucked into the narrow Tiber Valley.

Views down to Pieve Santo Stefano, tucked into the narrow, upper valley of the Tiber River

The parish church of Santo Stefano on the piazza of the same name

PIEVE SANTO STEFANO 431M POP 3249

Pieve Santo Stefano sits in the Upper Tiber River Valley at the foot of the mountains around Santuario della Verna. When the Nazis destroyed Pieve Santo Stefano in August 1944 in their northerly retreat from the Allied forces, they left the town without its former charming medieval character.

Today it is known as the 'City of the Diary' for the archive of over 7000 journals and diaries gathered by journalist Saverio Tutino as a sort of memorial to the daily lives of ordinary people. The archive can be visited at Piazza Pellegrini Plinio, 1 (www.archiviodiari.it).

The lead-domed 17th-century church on the south side of town, Madonna dei Lumi, is the starting point for the town's annual celebration of light, held on 7–8 September.

Just 1km before Santo Stefano is B&B Il Castellare (Strada La Verna 20, tel 0575 799393, info@ilcastellare.eu, €30/50 includes breakfast). The 3-star Hotel Santo Stefano (Via Tiberina 95, tel 0575 797129, info@hotelsantostefanoarezzo.it, €55/85 or ask for pilgrim price, includes breakfast) is convenient to the center city. The Euro Hotel (Superstrada E45, tel 0575 797055, info@hotel-euro.it, €50/75 includes breakfast) is 1km south of town and on the highway, but is also right on the next day's walking route. The parish church of Santo Stefano has three beds for emergencies (tel 0575 799050).

STAGE 8
Pieve Santo Stefano to Sansepolcro

Start	Piazza Santo Stefano
Finish	Sansepolcro Cattedrale
Distance	25km
Total ascent	447m
Total descent	539m
Difficulty	Moderate
Duration	8hrs
Note	The only services come just 3km before the end, so bring along plenty of food and water.

The Auto Strada has consumed the traditional road through the Tiber Valley between Pieve Santo Stefano and Sansepolcro, so the official Via di Francesco track goes east of the highway over the mountains to connect the two in a grueling 36km day. Instead, this track leads west of Lago Montedoglio and reaches the goal in 11 fewer kilometers. After following roads to the Euro Hotel the track leads up into the hills, enjoying wide views of the surrounding region before descending onto quiet country roads to enter Sansepolcro from the south.

Begin at the Piazza Santo Stefano and, facing the church, go left. In one block turn right just before the arch onto

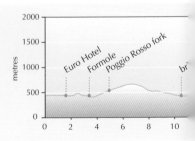

Via Arezzo and walk toward the wide automobile street. Once at the Via Tiberina turn left and follow signs to the Euro Hotel. In 150m is a small, triangular park just before the river. Turn right here and then immediately right again. Cross a small creek and follow the road to the left.

The road turns to gravel, then comes alongside the wall of the Auto Strada Statale 3bis. Follow this straight ahead, and in about 800m the road turns right and goes under the freeway then turns left again along the highway's opposite side. Go past the truck stop and to the back of the **Euro Hotel** and look for a sign that says 'Trail 22: 15.5km.' Pick up the two-track gravel road just after the hotel, going uphill and to the right.

Soon the road comes to a clearing; afterward, when the track seems to go uphill to the right, look instead for the hidden path on the left that traverses the mountainside. The river is now just below. ▸ A trail intersects soon and you turn right on it, going uphill. Turn left when the road comes to an intersection with a gravel road, carefully walking downhill as the road quickly becomes quite steep. Pass a gravel quarry and in another 300m turn right on the asphalt road. You soon arrive at the small settlement of **Formole** with its equestrian facilities on the left and right.

Just after the barricade in 400m turn right on a gravel road that goes uphill. Continue for 1.2km past a few vacation homes on the left to the second of two summits. Go right at the **fork** in the direction of Poggio Rosso and for 5.5km follow this quiet gravel road among pastures

In 2015 this hillside was logged. The trail may now be harder to follow.

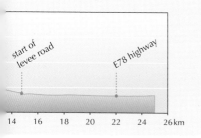

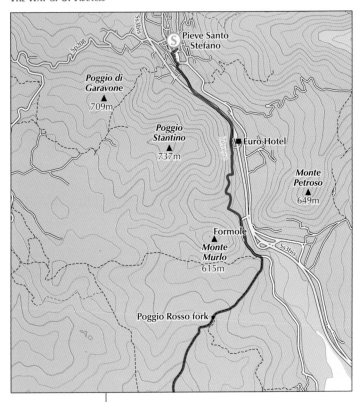

and forests along the ridgeline, enjoying vistas to the right of La Verna and Caprese Michelangelo. After a time the road descends, comes to some houses and then soon afterward arrives at a stop sign at an asphalt road (Strada Provinciale 48) at the bottom of the hill.

Turn right here and continue 400m to the concrete **bridge** across an arm of the Lago Montedoglio reservoir (10.5km). Cross the bridge and continue on the quiet country road for 1.6km. Follow the CAI markers and green arrows and turn left at the next asphalt road, **Strada Provinciale 47**.

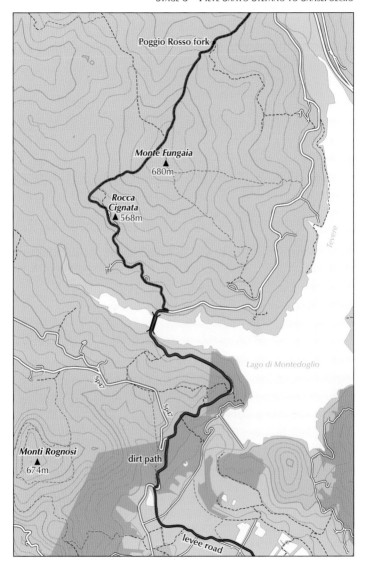

Poggio Rosso fork

Monte Fungaia
▲
680m

Rocca
Cignata
▲ 568m

Tevere

Lago di Montedoglio

Sp47

Sp47

Monti Rognosi
▲
674m

dirt path

levee road

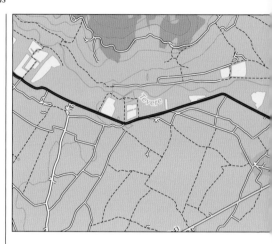

Follow this highway for 800m until turning left just after the guardrail of a curve onto a **dirt path** under power lines. Go downhill past an iron gate, cross the road, and go straight on a gravel farm road between two fields, following the CAI 14 and green arrow markers. Now you are atop a **levee** (bank) with the Tiber (Tevere) River on your left.

Continue straight on this flat gravel road for 3.3km, where it turns briefly to asphalt. Just after a small collection of homes on the left the asphalt road veers to the right. Take the gravel fork to the left here, following the green arrows. Soon the road veers toward the right and in another 700m a gravel crushing facility appears on the left. The road turns to asphalt in 1km and, just as the road comes to an end, turn left at the fork, which leads toward the outskirts of the industrial town of **Santa Fiora**.

Just after crossing the bridge you will find a gas station and café/bar on the left, the first services since this morning's departure.

Cross a road and round a corner to the left onto Strada Provinciale dell Libbia, which then turns toward the right and ends at the **E78 highway** (22km). Since this highway's busy bridge is the only way to cross the Tiber on this side of Sansepolcro, turn left here. ◄

Continue on the highway again, heading for the Auto Strada bridge. Just before the underpass cross the highway and take the small gravel road that runs toward

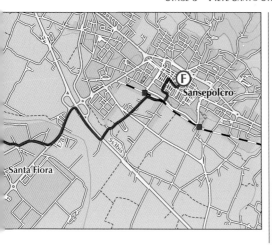

Exterior of Sansepolcro's co-cathedral of San Giovanni Evangelista

the right, next to the freeway. In 500m turn left and cross under the Auto Strada in the pedestrian tunnel.

Go straight ahead and gradually uphill, crossing three intersections, until the road takes a sharp turn to the right. Soon the road turns left and crosses railroad tracks. Continue straight ahead past a parking lot and through the city walls. Turn left just afterward onto Via Santa Croce and cross under an arch. Turn right at the next block, Via Lucca Pacioli, and after passing Albergo Fiorentino come to the main street of **Sansepolcro**, Via XX Settembre. Turn right and two blocks later, at Via Matteotti, arrive at the Cathedral of San Giovanni Evangelista and City Hall on the left.

SANSEPOLCRO 330M POP 16,109

The ancient name of Sansepolcro was 'Borgo of the Holy Sepulcher,' after its ninth-century monastery dedicated to the tomb of Christ. The town has long been an economic hub for the upper Tiber Valley and to this day its medieval center is filled with shops and restaurants. On market days the Via XX Settembre overflows with vendors selling their wares to local residents and tourists among the low, earthen-colored stucco buildings.

While St Francis traveled through here, stories of his presence focus on the nearby convent of Montecasale. Once some robbers were camped near the monastery and Francis' followers wondered what to do. He counseled them to take food to the robbers and speak words of grace. Surprised to receive such good treatment, the bandits soon were carrying firewood to the monastery to return the brothers' kindness. Not long afterward they gave up their criminal ways and some later even became followers.

Another story tells of two young men who approached Francis at the convent, hoping to join the friars. Francis gave them both the same task – to go to the garden and plant two cabbages upside down with their roots facing up. Son of a farmer, the first objected to the task as poor horticulture. The second did as Francis said. Francis sent the first back to his home to use his gifts as a good farmer while the other Francis welcomed into the brotherhood as a humble and obedient follower.

The remote location of quiet and serene Montecasale has allowed it to remain relatively untouched for centuries, and it remains a beautiful and spiritual place. Now home to Capucin monks, the monastery is an arduous walk but only a 15-minute taxi ride from Central Sansepolcro. (Servizio Taxi No 1, tel 335 5234282, info@sansepolcrotaxi.it, €25.)

The convenient Albergo Fiorentino (Via Luca Pacioli 56, tel 0575 740350, info@albergofiorentino.com, €55/80) is just off the main street of the old city. Less expensive but outside the historic center is Relais Oroscopo (Via Togliatti 68, tel 0575 734875, info@relaisoroscopo.com, €45/70). The Cathedral has five guest rooms, two with bathrooms en suite, in the Foresteria at the former convent of Santa Maria dei Servi (Piazza Dotti 2, tel 0575 742347, info@santamariadeiservi.it, €22).

STAGE 9

Sansepolcro to Citerna

Start	Sansepolcro Duomo
Finish	Main piazza, Citerna
Distance	12.5km
Total ascent	280m
Total descent	124m
Difficulty	Easy
Duration	4hrs

Until a final climb, this is a short and very flat stage through urban streets, warehouse districts and farms on the way to the tiny but very charming hill town of Citerna. It may be best to consider Citerna a pleasant lunch and provisioning stop because the town presently has no lodging in its boundaries. However, just 1km before is the spartan Convento Zoccolanti, while 1km afterward is Poggio Villa Fano, and in another 5.5km is Agriturismo Le Burgne. Citerna is worth a stop, though, for its quaint charm and majestic views of the Tiber Valley.

The safest choice for leaving Sansepolcro is to retrace your steps from yesterday back over the railroad tracks

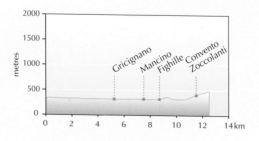

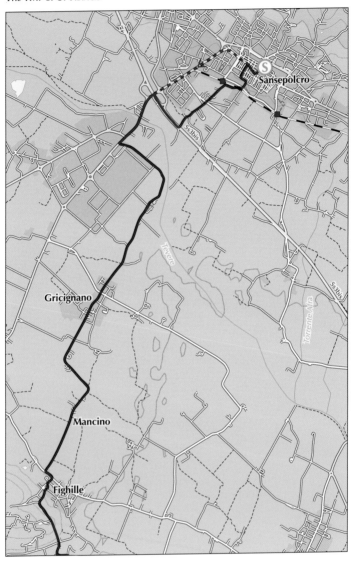

and under the autostrada to the **Strada Statale 3bis**. However, if you have shopping to do, the following variation may be useful.

Via Sansepolcro center

Start at the cathedral and turn left, walking the Via Matteotti to Via XX Settembre. Turn right and walk along the shops and hotels, through the archway of the city walls and straight ahead. In two blocks the road veers left and becomes Via dei Lorena. Follow this automobile road straight downhill toward the Strada Statale 3bis. Just before the freeway, carefully cross the traffic circle on the right side, across from an unusual modern church, and dodge traffic as you make your way under the freeway overpass, aiming toward the gas station and café/bar ahead in two blocks.

Continue along the busy road and cross the Tiber River on the familiar auto bridge. After the commercial district turn left onto Strada Vicinale Reglia dei Molini. Follow this long, flat road through a mixture of warehouses, factories and farms, as it becomes Via Tevere. ▶ Continue along the road through the town of **Gricignano** (5.3km) and go straight at the next intersection, where you enter the Region of Umbria.

Citerna now becomes visible on the hilltop straight ahead, and in a few hundred meters you come to the tiny settlement of **Mancino** (7.7km). Pass the pilgrim-friendly but posh Relais Antonella (www.relaisantonella.com, tel 075 8592838, from €70) and after leaving Mancino go left briefly on the Strada Provinciale 100 toward the town of **Fighille** (8.6km). In 100m turn right on Via Gabriotti and left onto Via del Pozzo. Wind your way up toward the café/bar, which serves the Centro Sportico swimming pool and sports complex behind it.

After the sports complex continue uphill and veer left towards the cemetery at the next fork, with Stations of the Cross guiding the way. Come to the gate of a villa and go to the left of it, heading downhill along a green chain link fence. After the fence, continue down the narrow path toward the asphalt road.

Note the factory and world headquarters of Buitoni Pasta on the right.

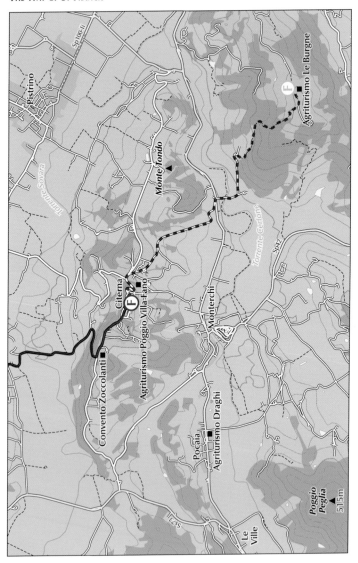

Cross the asphalt road and go straight. Continue on this road as it heads toward the hill on which you can now clearly see the town of Citerna. Stay on this asphalt road through switchbacks as it climbs the hill. Partway up the hill the waymarks suggest a path to the right, but the path is actually longer whereas this road is fairly quiet and more direct.

Soon a road joins from the right and across you see **Convento Zoccolanti**. Pass the convent on your right and continue the ascent as you come to the first homes of **Citerna** and a view of the valley through trees to the left. Continue past the large stone wall on the right and come to the tiny and charming piazza of Citerna, with its panoramic view on the left, its clock tower, the Chiesa di San Michele Arcangel and the town's bars and upscale restaurant.

(For directions to nearby accommodation along the next stage of the route, see the start of Stage 10, below.)

Main street of Citerna

CITERNA 480M POP 3332

The city walls of the hilltop town of Citerna, built in the 13th and 14th centuries, denote its prior existence as a fortress, guarding from its heights the strategic Upper Tiber Valley. Perched at the top is a citadel area that still has a system of defensive walkways and underground cisterns for rainwater. The monastery of St Elizabeth, at the far end of town, features a 14th-century German pieta, but in the Church of San Francesco and the Church of Archangel Michael 15th-century terra cottas of the Madonna and Child by Donatello and Robbia were recently discovered.

Above the town square is a clock tower that includes wooden pieces from the 16th century. Across from the tower in the main piazza is a viewpoint from which you can see to Sansepolcro and as far as the high peak of Mount Penna, site of Santuario della Verna.

Convento Zoccolanti (Zoccolanti 8, info@osbciterna.com, by donation; linens or sleeping bag required; kitchen available but bring your own food). You may also be able to find the parish priest, who has rooms available for pilgrims (Don Paolo, tel 0758 592708). Another option just outside town is the agriturismo Poggio Villa Fano (700m past the city gate, tel 347 0834295, info@poggiodivillafano.it) with kitchens in each apartment and a lovely outdoor swimming pool. Agriturismo Draghi (Via Pocaia 64, tel 575 70169, €30/50, plus €5 breakfast) is 3km away, beyond the town of Monterchi. You may also choose to continue on tomorrow's itinerary 5.5km to Agriturismo Le Burgne (tel 0758 502020, www.agriturismole-burgne.it, €72, plus €7 breakfast).

STAGE 10
Citerna to Città di Castello

Start	Main piazza, Citerna
Finish	Duomo, Città di Castello
Distance	20.3km
Total ascent	816m
Total descent	938m
Difficulty	Moderate
Duration	7hrs 30mins
Note	Stock up at Citerna since the only place to purchase food or water is very near the day's end.

Today's deceptively long stage crosses three tall ridges that separate fertile valleys and farmlands, before finishing in a long downhill walk to charming Città di Castello. A sometimes-treacherous option along the highway from Lerchi can shorten the stage.

Standing in the tiny main piazza of Citerna with the panoramic view at your back, turn left on Corso Garibaldi and go downhill. Pass under the arch, by the Municipio and then past the Monastero di Santa Elisabetta. After going through the city gate turn left and follow the winding road down to the main auto road. Turn right at the first fork, where you see the driveway sign for Poggio Villa Fano on the left.

Turn right again at the tiny chapel, continuing downhill among farms and pastures with views of the village of Monterchi to the right. Follow the road to the bottom of the valley and turn left onto the **Strada Statale 221** (2.5km). Stay on the highway for just 60m and then turn right onto a gravel road.

Follow the gravel road across a creek and 175m later turn left, beginning an ascent that becomes steeper in a few hundred meters. The curvy road continues between hayfields and along woods as it makes its way to the top of the hill. In 1.2km, after going through some woods, turn right at an unmarked junction.

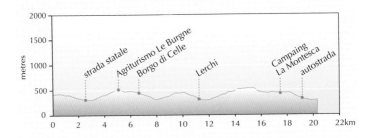

107

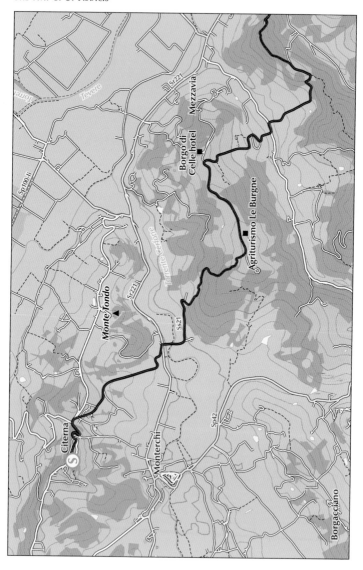

At the top of the hill, turn left on the gravel road. ▶ Soon you come to **Agriturismo Le Burgne**, which is available for breakfast, coffee and snacks. After leaving the agriturismo do not be distracted by red-and-white markers; instead continue on the same gravel road along the ridge, as the road goes gently downhill then uphill once again.

From this height you can see back to Citerna, Sansepolcro and beyond.

Come to a summit in 1.2km and 300m later the gravel road ends at an asphalt road with a stylish hotel, the **Borgo di Celle**, just ahead. Turn right, heading downhill, and follow the asphalt road for 1.1km to the bottom of the valley. ▶

From here you can see to the right the imposing 11th-century Monte Santa Maria Tiberina castle.

At the bottom of the valley turn left on the asphalt road and 100m later turn right onto a gravel road. Head uphill and 600m later take a sharp turn to the left. In 300m, after a steep uphill climb, come to a barbed wire gate. Go through the gate and turn left; after about 200m you come to a high point from which you can see parts of the town of Lerchi at the bottom of the valley.

The Castle of Santa Maria Tibertina in the distance

109

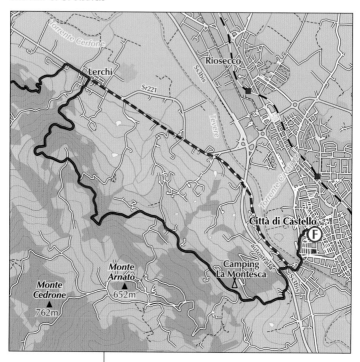

Continue past the summit as the road turns from asphalt to gravel and follow the ridge through a forest of small pines. Near the top of the hill, take the fork to the right that continues uphill and a few minutes later come to the very top of the ridge.

After the house at the top of the ridge the gravel road descends steeply. In 100m, at a confusing intersection, turn right onto a driveway going downhill. At a second driveway take the path that parallels it to the left, going steeply downhill. At the bottom of the dirt path you come to a field and then a vineyard; in 50m, after a large tree, turn right on a two-track gravel drive.

Take this road to the asphalt road at the bottom of the valley, then turn left. The asphalt road soon crosses a creek and in a moment comes to the outskirts of **Lerchi** (11.4km). Turn right onto a suburban road between two-story homes. ▶

Shortcut to Città di Castello

If you want to shorten your day by walking the highway option, aim toward the Hotel Boschetto where you pick up the main route that joins from the right after crossing under the Auto Strada. Bear in mind, however, that the busy highway can make for an unpleasant walking experience and great care should be taken. (Or, if your day has already been too long, another option is to take the SI381 bus into town, which runs every couple of hours.)

In 100m the waymarks point you toward the right – uphill and away from town. Soon the asphalt ends on a well-graded gravel road, which at first climbs steeply and then more gently. At the iron gate of a large villa turn right onto a two-track gravel road that continues uphill.

Soon you come to a fork where you turn left and begin a gradual downhill past a small shrine. In five minutes leave a gate to the right and follow a stone wall next

If you walk toward the church tower in one block you will find a café/bar for refreshment as well as the main highway into Città di Castello.

Cathedral of Saints Florido and Amanzio in Città di Castello

111

to the gate around the left side of a large house. Wind down through the driveway toward the left and then continue downhill; patches of asphalt begin to appear and then you reach an intersection with an asphalt road. Turn right, then go straight at the next fork where soon you can look down on Città di Castello.

Stay on the asphalt road until, in about 10mins, you arrive at **Camping La Montesca** with its restaurant/pizzeria, mini-market and bar available for welcome refreshment. Continue along the asphalt road to a fork and go left, downhill toward the city. Soon you come to another fork where you go right, toward the front gate of a pinkish villa. The road now goes downhill steeply, passing large homes and a few scattered orchards where it finally turns right and crosses under the **Auto Strada** (19.3km).

At the bottom of the hill turn right on Via Cortonese and then take the first left. Cross the Tiber River on a bridge in 150m and continue straight to the traffic circle, which you follow to the left. In 100m go right at the fork, walking uphill and inside **Città di Castello**'s old city walls. At the end of this lane is a small staircase leading to a Vittorio Emmanuel statue in a park across from the lovely 11th-century Cattedrale dei Santi Florido e Amanzio, just across the piazza.

Town hall and Piazza Matteotti

CITTÀ DI CASTELLO 288M POP 40,479

The Umbrian people established Città di Castello on the banks of the Tiber River over 2500 years ago. Continuously occupied since then, the town was rebuilt and fortified by its bishop, Floridus, around a new castle, ultimately earning it the name Città di Castello. Its medieval walls, many of which survive, date to the 14th and 15th centuries.

Towering above the town's buildings are the 11th-century Torre Comunale and the cathedral's 12th-century Campanile Cilindrico. The town is a center for medieval and Renaissance art and its Pinacoteca Comunale art gallery has significant works from Ghiberti, Signorelli, Raphael and della Robbia. The cathedral's museum houses a collection of Christian art, including a display of 25 rare objects from the sixth century used for Eucharistic liturgy that were found while plowing a nearby field in 1935. The museum also houses the 'Dragon's Bone,' found in nearby Pietralunga and transported here as evidence of dragons – or at least of dinosaurs.

Thomas of Celano reports in his biography of Francis that a woman possessed by a devil lived in town and caused a great deal of disturbance to the inhabitants. While Francis was visiting locally the inhabitants implored him to call on this woman and cast out her demon. Francis sent one of the brothers instead and, on meeting the woman, the demon began to mock the brother, knowing he was not Francis. After hearing this Francis himself came to the woman, who immediately upon seeing him began to tremble violently. Francis shouted to the demon to come out – but nothing appeared to have happened. Francis' embarrassment was so great that he immediately left town, ashamed at his failure. The next time he came to town, though, the cured woman sought him out and thanked him for saving her life. She threw herself at his feet and kissed his footprints until she finally was able to reassure him that his earlier ministry to her had been a success. Celano reports that the momentary embarrassment helped Francis accept the gift of humility, reminding him that it was God's power, not his own, which enabled any miracles.

It is hard to imagine powerful demons and embarrassed saints among the warm brick-and-umber tones of today's Città di Castello. The town has a lively street life among its cafés, bars and restaurants. The local bread, cooked below the ashes of the oven, is called *ciacia* (pronounced 'cha-cha'), and is used to make handheld pizza-like sandwiches.

Hotel Umbria (Via S Antonio, tel 075 8554925, umbria@hotelumbria.net, €45) is in the heart of the old town and caters to pilgrims. Also convenient, although more expensive, is the historic Hotel Tiferno (Piazza R Sanzio 13, tel 075 8550331, info@hoteltiferno.it, €60/90). Residenze Antica Canonica (Via San Florido 23, tel 075 8523298, info@anticacanonica.it, from €20) offers rooms with 2–8 beds to pilgrims.

STAGE 11
Città di Castello to Pietralunga

Start	Duomo, Città di Castello
Finish	Main piazza, Pietralunga
Distance	29.8km
Total ascent	889m
Total descent	607m
Difficulty	Moderate
Duration	8hrs 30mins
Note	There is one bar/café a few kilometers outside Città, but it is best to bring enough food and water for a long day of walking.

Start early for this long but scenic stage that climbs along pastures and pine forests to the delightful village of Pietralunga in the Chiascio River drainage. A stay at Candeggio (13.3km) or Pieve di Saddi (18.5km) hostels, or at Agriturismo Il Pioppa Casa (23km) can shorten the day.

Facing the front door of the cathedral, follow its left side along Corso Cavour. In a few blocks make a right turn onto Corso Vittorio Emanuele. Cross under the archway

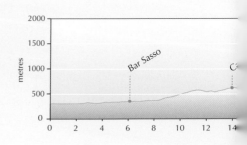

of the city walls and go straight ahead. The road now becomes Via Rignaldello, which you follow until it curves left and comes to an intersection at Viale Orlando. Turn right and a block later take the right fork. In 500m take a left turn and three blocks later, after the railroad tracks, turn right onto Vocabolo Prima Baucca.

Follow this quiet paved road as it begins a gentle climb toward the mountains. Resist any deviations, but in 1.7km at **Baucca** take the left fork, which briefly leads around a narrow section that is somewhat dangerous for pedestrians. In 2.3km come to **Bar Sasso** (6.1km), which is the last bar until Pietralunga. ▶

Across the street you may enjoy the park and its gentle cascade of water over bedrock.

Continue on the road for 1.8km then turn right, as marked, onto a gravel drive. In 150m you cross a creek and at the following fork go left and uphill. The gravel road now climbs, first through fields and then through woods on a series of switchbacks. In 2km come to an asphalt road, turn right and 400m later arrive at a small store that carries local specialty goods.

Stay on the asphalt road and continue 500m to the first summit. Begin a descent just afterward and in 1km come to a low point where another ascent begins. A number of paths take off to the left and right, but stay on the asphalt road for the next 1.4km until you come to a small and hospitable park with log benches and a fountain on the right (14km). The pilgrim hostel 'Cammino di Pace' at **Candeggio** (tel 075 8526282, info@chepasso. org, €3) is just 150m to the right.

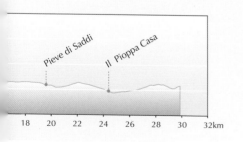

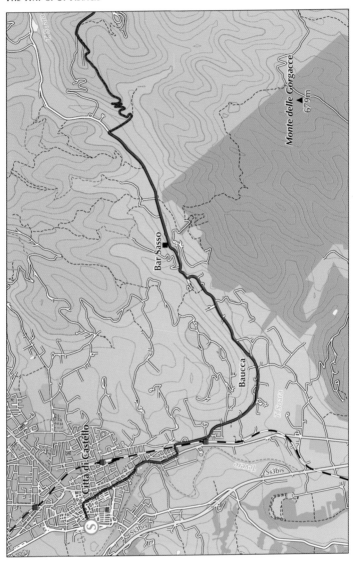

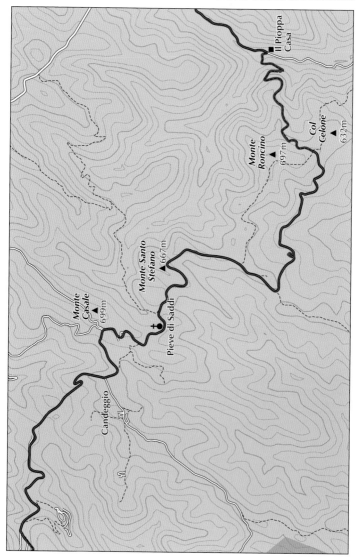

Il Pioppa Casa

Col Celone
▲ 632m

Monte Roncino
▲ 697m

Monte Santo Stefano
▲ 667m

Monte Casale
▲ 699m

Pieve di Saddi

Candeggio

Continue on the asphalt road, ignoring all other options, including an intersection at 850m with a sign pointing left to Pietralunga. Instead, follow the waymarks on this same asphalt road and in 300m come to the summit of **Monte Santo Stefano** (667m) where you can look down to the right toward Candeggio.

Continue on the asphalt road for another 3.9km until you begin a descent. Turn left at a fork, and come to the fourth-century church of **Pieve di Saddi** (19.7km) with its adjoining pilgrim hostel (tel 349 8119975, pievedesaddi@gmail.com). Even if you choose not to stay here it is still worth a knock on the door to investigate the ancient church's frescoes.

Continue on the asphalt road and in 2.5km reach a summit where paths branch to the left and right. Go straight ahead and begin a descent. In 2.2km at a hairpin turn come to the driveway for agriturismo **Il Pioppa Casa** (tel 368 7366512, info@ilpioppocasevacanze.com, €18/22 includes kitchen but no food).

Continue downhill along the asphalt road, crossing a creek over a bridge with an iron railing. About 2.9km after the turn for Il Pioppa Casa you finish a long uphill climb and the road merges with another road coming from the right. Go left (straight) on this new road; you can now look down to Pietralunga on the right.

*View of Pietralunga
from the trail above*

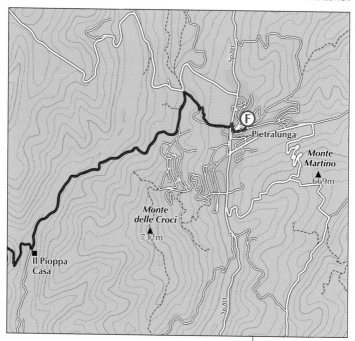

After 400m the road comes to a stop sign, but 30m before the sign turn right, going downhill. In 250m turn left, off the asphalt, onto a two-track dirt road that goes downhill and becomes an asphalt driveway between two two-story homes. The drive continues to the right but at an intersection in 100m turn left onto an asphalt road that leads to the floor of the valley.

When the road makes a sharp turn to the right go straight instead and take a stairway up to the main road, Via Bruno Buozzi. Go left along the road, cross it, and immediately turn right (uphill) onto a narrow street that takes you on switchbacks and stairways through the old village and up to the main piazza of **Pietralunga** with its eighth- to 10th-century Pieve di Santa Maria and eighth-century Rocca tower.

PIETRALUNGA 566M POP 2270

Enjoy the charming old town of Pietralunga on your way to the historic Church of Santa Maria and citadel tower on the main piazza. Crowded into the narrow streets are the 18th-century former hospital, 15th-century Captain's Palace, and 12th-century convent.

The town was established by the Umbrians and inhabited continuously, except for the sixth to seventh centuries after the Goths overwhelmed and destroyed it. By the eighth century it was rebuilt and became part of the Lombard reign, later to be aligned with Città di Castello, the Papal States and finally the Kingdom of Italy. More than 100 soldiers from Pietralunga perished in World War I, and in the Second World War Pietralunga was a center of the Anti-Fascist resistance movement.

Renovated in about 2004, the Hotel Tinca (Via Guglielmo Marconi 7, tel 0759 460057, info@hotel-tinca.com, €35/70) feels fresh and modern and has good views to the west. The Parrochia di Santa Maria has pilgrim beds as well (tel 075 9460055).

STAGE 12
Pietralunga to Gubbio

Start	Main piazza, Pietralunga
Finish	Piazza San Giovanni, Gubbio
Distance	26.5km
Total ascent	784m
Total descent	760m
Difficulty	Moderate
Duration	8hrs
Note	No services available, so plan to carry adequate food and water for the day's hike.

The first half of the day is on quiet roads and sometimes-steep paths in the forested mountains, while the second half is along fields of hay and sunflowers as you approach the picturesque and ancient town of Gubbio. An early start to the day allows more time to enjoy this popular and historic town.

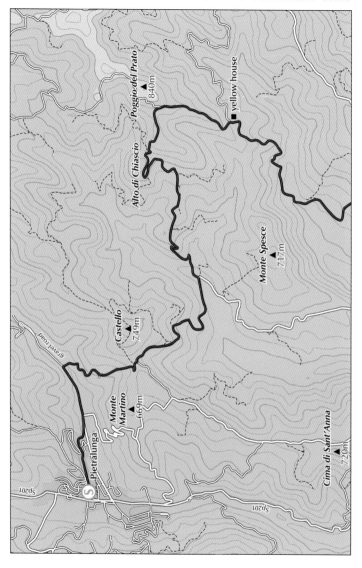

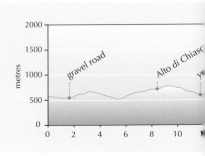

From the main piazza of Pietralunga follow the road between the pizzeria and grocery, the Via Roma, downhill. In 900m, at a fork in the road, go straight, following the signs to Gubbio. In another 800m, at the bottom of the hill, go straight again, leaving the main road for the Via Caipatrignani. Turn right in 700m at a **gravel road** that appears on the right. Soon come to the bed of a seasonal creek and afterward a fork in the road; take the right fork and begin the first climb of the day.

A house appears on the right in 700m. Go straight on the gravel road in front of the house and afterward begin a gentle climb toward the hill. In 200m the climb becomes steeper and in a few minutes stay left, following the stone marker, as a gravel road takes off to the right. In 100m take the asphalt road that goes toward the right and then turn left at the fork that comes immediately after. Follow this asphalt road for the next 2.3km as it goes downhill and crosses a small creek.

Just after the creek turn left onto a gravel road that begins a slow uphill climb. Follow this road for 1.7km as it climbs past a large derelict house surrounded by a fence. Continue for 300m and go straight at the intersection. After 600m go uphill at the fork. Partway up the hill see the sign on the left describing the many trails in this area, the **Alto di Chiascio**.

In a few minutes you come to a small reservoir where just afterwards you turn right. The road now climbs steeply to a summit in 200m. In 400m at a hairpin turn,

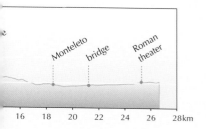

instead of going left go straight ahead onto another gravel road that leads in a southerly direction through a logging area. A long descent begins here and leftward vistas open over hayfields to the valley below.

In 500m turn right at the fork and head toward a **yellow house** that has been visible for some time. Walk past the house (10.8km) and continue to a second yellow house, walking between it and its barn. Continue left at the next fork and then continue straight further on as a gravel road joins from the left. In 500m the road suddenly turns to asphalt and heads up a steep hill.

In another 500m the flat and wide Chiascio Valley floor can be seen ahead. Soon the road levels out and begins to hug the sheer mountainside of pinkish orange stone, traversing the slope as the road gently descends to the valley floor below.

After a time the track turns suddenly right and down a steep hill between two houses. In 600m, as the houses grow more numerous, the road is joined by another asphalt road from the right. Cross a creek in 500m and continue along the road to an intersection 100m ahead. Turn left and 40m later turn right and take a short climb back up the hill. Views of the wide valley floor become clearer now, with the Auto Strada piercing its basin below.

Soon you come to the tiny settlement of **Monteleto** (18.2km), with its parish church on the left. Continue on the asphalt road above the town's main street, passing

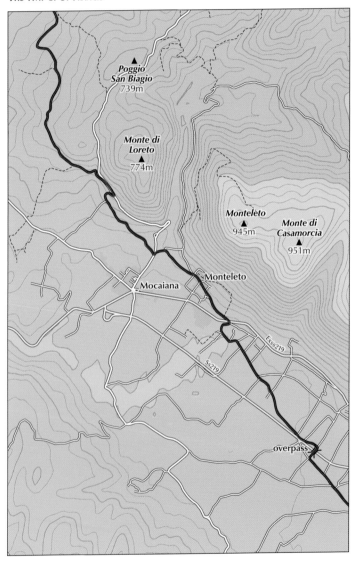

the cemetery. In 700m carefully cross the Strada Statale. Just after crossing, turn left and then immediately right. At the next fork, just after a green chain link fence, turn left onto a gravel road. There is immediately another fork in the road: turn left onto this dirt road leading through hayfields.

Soon you come to an asphalt road. Turn right here and follow it for 700m to an intersection with another asphalt road. Go straight toward the freeway on this road, avoiding all turns for the next 1.5km where it nears the SS219 Auto Strada.

A city street in old Gubbio

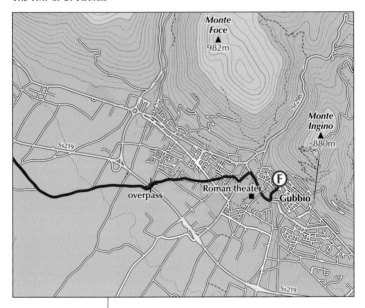

Turn right onto the new **freeway overpass bridge** (21.5km) and then turn left onto the same road that would have continued straight if not for being bisected by the Auto Strada. Gubbio now appears plainly on the mountainside to the left.

In 1km continue over a small rise at a canal crossing; go straight and follow the same road for the next 1.5km where it again crosses the Auto Strada. Continue after the **freeway bridge** for 500m, noting the café/bar to the left adjacent to a large medical clinic, until you come to Via Leonardo da Vinci, which marks the beginning of the residential suburbs of Gubbio.

Although the red-and-white markers suggest turning right, instead go straight on the Via dell'Arborito for two blocks and turn right at the shopping area with the arched arcade. In one block you come to Viale Parrucchi, and across it is the park that holds Gubbio's impressive first-century **Roman Theater**. If you are able, this is a good time to visit this treasure since otherwise it is inconvenient to the center of Gubbio.

Turn left at the park and in two blocks go right at the roundabout just outside the city walls. Follow the Viale Teatro Romano along the outside of the city walls to the next automobile entry into the city walls, the Via Repubblica. Turn left into the city walls and arrive at the Chiesa di San Francesco on the left. Go through the parking lot opposite the church, past the news kiosk and up the street toward the delightful center city of **Gubbio**. The convenient Piazza San Giovanni is in just a few blocks, on the left side.

GUBBIO 522M POP 32,998

Palazzo dei Consoli and the Piazza Grande

Gubbio is one of Umbria's most beloved municipalities and is emblematic of the historic hill towns that cling to the mountainsides of Central Italy. Its rich and long history, its scenic beauty and its unique architectural character make it a highlight for tourists and pilgrims.

Gubbio traces its roots to the ancient Umbrian people. In 1444 a set of third- to first-century BC bronze tablets inscribed in Umbrian and Latin were discovered nearby. The tablets are the most important source of information about the Umbrian language, civilization and religious practices. The seven tablets can be viewed at the Civic Museum in the Palazzo dei Consoli.

By the second century BC, Gubbio (Roman Iguvium) was under the control of Rome. Their amphitheater is one of the largest extant Roman amphitheaters in the world and testifies to the importance of the city in Roman times.

In the Middle Ages Gubbio sent 1000 knights to fight in the First Crusade and, according to local legend, these knights were the first to enter the Church of the Holy Sepulcher when Jerusalem was captured in 1099. Many buildings in the old town come from the 14th–15th centuries, giving Gubbio a distinctly medieval aspect, although it may seem somewhat austere due to the greyish color of the local stone used in construction. The town is especially steep, and a series of pedestrian escalators and elevators allow easier access from the lower town to the main piazza, and above it to the cathedral.

A tour of Gubbio from bottom to top should include at least the Roman Theater, the 13th-century Church of San Francesco, the 14th-century Palazzo dei Consoli with its museum on the Piazza Grande, and the 12th-century Duomo with its many works of sacred art and stunning rose window. Not to be missed is the Funivia Colle Eletto, an open-air funicular that takes you in a standing basket to the Basilica di Sant'Ubaldo and its lovely gardens and restaurant.

All Italy knows of the Corsa dei Ceri, an annual race in Gubbio held each year on 15 May. On that day three teams of colorfully clad local supporters race up the city streets from Piazza Grande to the Basilica di Sant'Ubaldo carrying a trio of 4-meter tall, 280kg columns. Each heavy column has at its crown a statute of one of the saints. Tourists from throughout Italy and beyond fill the streets to cheer on the teams.

After his estrangement from his parents, Francis left Assisi with only a rude robe given him by Bishop Guido. He walked north through the frozen mountains and forests, feeling his first experience of deprivation and solitude in the snowy hills. Finally arriving at Gubbio, he was taken in at the home of his friend, Giacomo Spadalunga – now site of the Church of San Francesco. Here Francis began ministry to a nearby leper colony, and soon the new direction of his life was set.

One option is Grotta dell'Angelo Hotel (Via Gioia 47, tel 075 9271747, info@grottadellangelo.it, from €38/50 plus €5 for breakfast). Very convenient but slightly more expensive is highly rated Hotel Gattapone (Via Beni 11, tel 075 9272489, info@hotelgattapone.net), just off Piazza San Giovanni. Four double rooms are available above La Locanda del Cantiniere restaurant (Via Dante 30, tel 075 9275999, info@locandadelcantiniere.it), which also offers a pilgrims' menu. Several parishes and religious orders have housing available for pilgrims. Instituto Maestre Pie Filippini is well maintained by the nuns, with 17 beds in clean rooms (Corso Garibaldi 102, tel 075 9273768, maestrepiefgubbio@virgilio.it). Madonna del Prato parish (Via Perugina 94, tel 075 9274574, madonnadelprato@gmail.com) has small rooms with bunk beds, and Convento di San Secondo (Via Madonna del Ponte 4, tel 075 9273869, bilioteca.steuco@libero.it) has 40 spaces in 17 rooms.

STAGE 13
Gubbio to Biscina

Start	Piazza San Giovanni, Gubbio
Finish	Tenuto di Biscina
Distance	22.7km
Total ascent	895m
Total descent	688m
Difficulty	Moderate
Duration	8hrs
Note	Since there is no large town in the 38.5km stretch between Gubbio and Valfabbrica, you may choose to finish the day at a number of agriturismi along the way, including Ponte di Riocchio (8.2km), Valdichiascio (11.4km) or Tenuto Biscina (22.7km).

This stage follows rolling and sometimes steep hills along parts of the trail between Gubbio and Assisi that St Francis walked in 1206–07 after his estrangement from his family. The undulating topography of the Chiascio Valley makes the region very scenic, and it is populated with small farms and agriturismi. Frequent fields, streams and forests make this a very green and pleasant walk.

Go downhill from the Piazza San Giovanni in the heart of Gubbio on the Via Repubblica, past the Piazza 40 Martiri, to the San Francesco church. Pass the church on its left side and then turn left at the stoplight just after the city walls onto Via Matteotti. Cross toward the gas station to get onto the gravel walk, following this road along the city walls. Soon you see a bank and a Saldi Sport store with hiking gear and other items that might be useful for hikers. In four long blocks, turn right onto Via Manzoni and follow the gravel walk downhill. In 300m are Via Frate Lupo and the sculpture and church that remember Francis and the wolf of Gubbio.

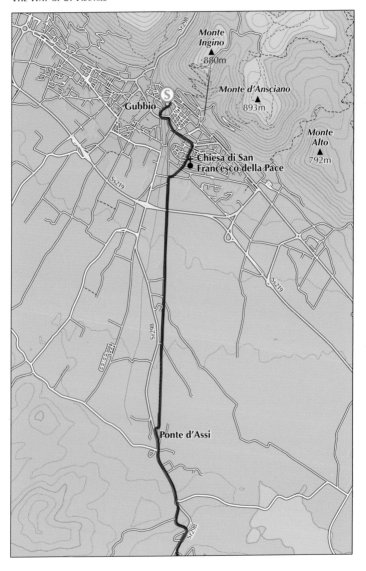

FRANCIS AND THE WOLF OF GUBBIO

During Francis' stay in Gubbio a marauding wolf was terrorizing the countryside. At first it targeted livestock, but soon it was hunting humans exclusively. The town and surrounding residents were terrified of the wolf and implored Francis to intervene. Francis approached the wolf's refuge with a small crowd following from a safe distance.

Upon seeing Francis, the wolf lunged with bared teeth, but when Francis made the sign of the cross the wolf stopped and listened. With the crowd watching in amazement, Francis spoke quietly with the wolf, which sat patiently at his feet. At the end of their talk the animal placed his paw in Francis' hand, as though to confirm an agreement.Francis and the wolf then walked together into town, and the wolf laid at his feet while Francis announced to the village that an agreement had been made: in exchange for daily food provided by its residents, the wolf would no longer harm any humans. Affirming the agreement in the presence of the villagers, the wolf once again placed his paw in Francis' hand. The townspeople complied, and each day the wolf went from house to house to receive food from the residents.

The wolf lived in peace with the village until its death two years later. When the wolf passed away, residents buried its body with honor at the small church of St Francis of the Peace outside the walls. In the renovation of the church in 1872 a wolf's skeleton was found under a slab outside the building. It was brought inside the church and placed under the altar, in memory of its transformation by the beloved saint.

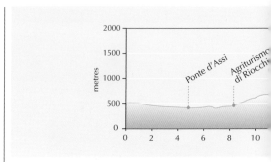

After a visit to the chapel, cross straight ahead in front of the church onto the pedestrian walk through the park. Turn right onto the arterial and then left at the next street. Follow the Via Piaggiola for 3.2km as it goes straight, first under the Strada Statale della Contessa (SS219), then past a 12th-century former leper hospital, along fields, past a soccer field, and then as it becomes an asphalt road. Turn right 600m later into a parking lot and walk across it toward a gas station, bar, fruit store and butcher shop on the highway in the town of **Ponte d'Assi**. ◀

This is a good place to stock up on supplies for the remainder of the stage.

With the stores at your back, turn right onto the sidewalk of the Strada Provinciale. Follow the highway for 900m until the road to San Ciprignano takes off to the right. Turn right here for a brief respite from the highway and then in 200m go straight on the left fork and return to the highway.

Back at the highway, turn right and follow it for 250m until you turn left in the direction of Agriturismo San Vittorino. Just after the left turn come to a fork and go right, toward **Agriturismo Ponte di Riocchio** (8.2km), which you reach in 1.2km. After the agriturismo the road continues uphill and to the right where you can look back for the first of many sweeping views of Gubbio.

The road continues up a long and sometimes steep hill for the next 2km until it ends at an asphalt road in a T-junction. Turn left and head toward the woods for another climb of about 100m in length. After the summit

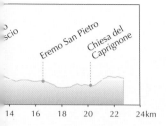

you come to a fork and turn right. Soon you arrive at **Agriturismo Valdichiascio** (11.4km) on the left.

Continue along the gravel road and in 600m come to a high point. Now you begin a long downhill. At a fork in 400m turn left and then go straight through a series of intersections for the next 2km until arriving at the **Madonna della Grazie shrine** with its large lawn. Begin a climb upward from here and in 2.1km come to the 15th-century **Eremo di San Pietro** in Vignetto, home of Father Basil Martin who offers spiritual guidance to pilgrims between services of prayer.

Shrine of Madonna della Grazie

133

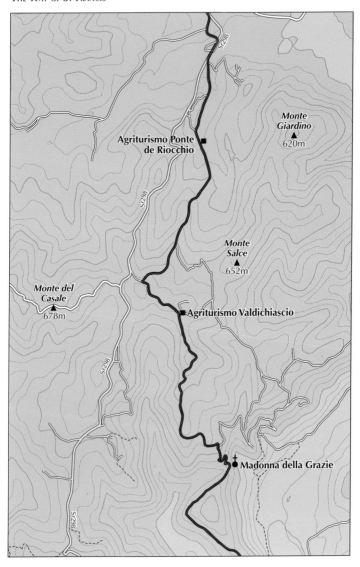

Turn left at the gates of the monastery and in 1.1km watch carefully as the track turns right onto a wide earthen path going downhill (17.7km). This offers a cross-country shortcut that avoids the many switchbacks of the gravel road.

In 350m come to a creek where the trail is washed out, and look carefully for an alternate creek crossing up and to the right. Cross the creek and continue uphill. Ahead and above you is an unusual pipeline bridge; turn left here and come to the crossing of another creek where two ropes are provided for handholds above the shallow current on its concrete sluiceway.

After the crossing pick up a two-track gravel road and in 100m turn right at a fork. Soon, go around a fence and uphill, where in 500m the trail ends at a wider gravel road. Turn left, going slightly downhill, and in 900m come to the 14th-century **Chiesa del Caprignone**, which offers a picnic table and park bench for a rest.

Continue on the path to the right, which narrows as it goes through the woods. In 200m cross a mildly sulfurous-smelling creek, after which the path goes uphill and

Ropes help in crossing the creek's concrete sluiceway

135

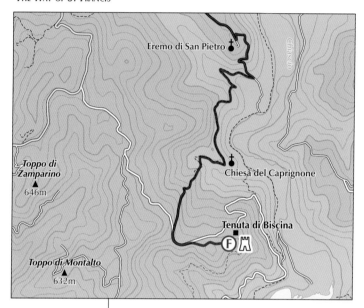

to the left. Very soon you come to a pasture with farm buildings above. Follow the fence up past the shepherd's quarters onto a driveway, and then continue up toward the house and garden.

Go between the posts of the stone wall toward the right and continue up the driveway. After the grey house veer left and look for waymarks. Soon you come to a sign for the dog 'Zanna' – a large black dog that can be unfriendly to pilgrims with walking sticks. Do not wave your hiking sticks, but instead – in a little St Francis-and-the-Wolf moment of your own – call softly to Zanna who then will pose no threat. In 100m come to an asphalt road and turn left.

Soon there is a fork in the road. Turn right onto the asphalt road and shortly see signs for Tenuta di Biscina (22.7km). At a fork in another 100m turn left and arrive at the pool, apartments and finally the reception area for the holiday apartment center.

BISCINA 731M POP 25

Situated equidistant between the rival powers of Gubbio, Assisi and Perugia, Biscina Castle (14th–16th-century) overlooks the strategic Chiascio Valley. Its name, similar to the word *biscia* – Italian for snake – may evoke the snake-like tendrils of the many mountainous arms of the region. At its height, the castle had a moat and drawbridge as defensive structures, along with the high tower still partly in existence today, giving it a view over many miles.

Directly on the trail, about halfway between Gubbio and Biscina, is Agriturismo Ponte di Riocchio (tel 075 9222611, pontediriocchio@libero.it, from €65, with triple and quad rooms available. Partial board €25). In a further 6km is the hospitality of delightful Maria Theresa at Agriturismo Valdichiascio (Frazione Valdichiascio 6, tel 075 920251, agriturismo@valdichiascio.net, €35 except August and festivals, plus half-board of €55), who takes extra care of pilgrims. Especially for families and weekly guests, Tenuta di Biscina (tel 075 9229730, info@biscina.it, double from €90. Ask for pilgrim prices) is a convenient option. Just 800m beyond is Agriturismo Sosta San Francesco (tel 333 3838769, direzione@lasostadisanfrancesco.com, €25).

STAGE 14
Biscina to Valfabbrica

Start	Tenuta di Biscina
Finish	Main piazza, Valfabbrica
Distance	15.9km
Total ascent	427m
Total descent	669m
Difficulty	Easy
Duration	5hrs

In this short stage through forests and along quiet country roads the route makes many twists and turns in order to pass around Lago di Valfabbrica. In theory, hardy walkers could combine this with the following stage and walk directly to Assisi in one day.

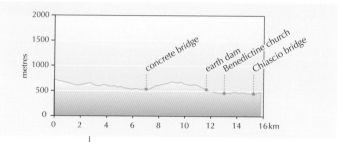

Leave the Biscina reception, going to the right on the road lined with cypress trees and noting the tower of Castello Biscina ahead. Follow the road as it circles down and around the castle and enjoy the spectacular views of the dam below on the Chiascio River. In 1.5km come to the bottom of the valley opposite the castle and begin walking uphill.

View of Lago di Valfabbrica and its earthen dam

In another 1.5km turn left on a path and follow wooden steps down to a creek. Cross the creek on stones and then continue up steps on the other side. In 200m go straight at the fork and just afterward come to a summit. After the summit be careful on the quick descent on gravel, clay soil and rock. Cross a creek and continue up

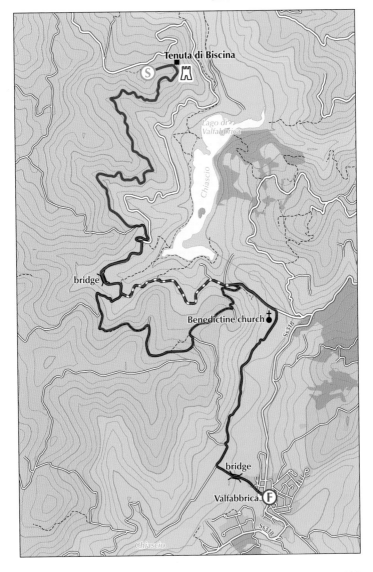

Tenuta di Biscina

Lago di Valfabbrica

Chiascio

bridge

Benedictine church

SS318

bridge

Valfabbrica

Chiascio

SS318

on the other side, then turn left and go downhill on the asphalt and gravel road that appears in 100m. At the wide and quiet asphalt road in 600m turn right.

Continue on the road and cross the **concrete bridge** that appears in 900m. In a further 500m a series of signs instruct you to turn right and go uphill. Here you have a choice: you can either stick to the official route, which takes a wide loop south before regaining the line of the Chiascio River, adding 3km to the day's journey and offering no new vistas, or you can cut the loop off by taking a more direct route on the asphalt road close to the dam.

The long way round
Go uphill past Agriturismo Borgo Sanbuco and the tiny adjacent church of San Marco. After the church take the right fork then watch carefully for a path that takes off to the left. Take the path and at the next intersection go uphill. Very soon after you come to a wooden cross, turn right on the gravel road. (Be careful for mud here in wet weather.)

After coming out of the forest in 600m you see a sign on the left for 'acqua potabile', pointing to a fountain beyond the cemetery below. You can either head down the hill directly to the cemetery or take the wide loop to the right on the official track, which lands you just below the cemetery at a small rest stop with (hopefully) a functioning water faucet and bench across from a small farmhouse and chicken coop.

Continue toward the small church, noting Valfabbrica in the distance on your right, and follow the road downhill past fields of carefully marked herbs and other crops. Just before Agriturismo Bellemonte turn left and go downhill. In 600m you arrive at the Strada Provinciale and the Lago di Valfabbrica Dam.

Shortcut
Instead of turning right, continue straight on the quiet asphalt road for 2.1km in the direction of Camere Villa Verde. The road passes the earthen Lago di Valfabbrica Dam and just after the dam the main route rejoins from the right.

Continue downhill along the now untamed Chiascio River and in 600m turn right before a bridge onto an asphalt road. Continue on this tractor road past the **Benedictine church** and then pass to the right of the farmhouse.

Sunflower fields outside Valfabbrica

In 1.5km the tractor road comes to an end at an asphalt road. Go left, following this road for 150m before taking another left. Head along fields, then under the new Auto Strada bridge (not shown on map). Cross the **Chiascio River bridge** and walk upward past sports fields into the town of **Valfabbrica**. The main piazza is just 500m uphill past the river.

VALFABBRICA 289M POP 3250

After Francis left Assisi in his self-exile from his family, he walked north toward Gubbio in the Chiascio. Although the weather was cold and the ground was covered in snow, Francis was singing happily to himself in French. When local bandits caught sight of him near the Chiesa di Caprignone they stopped him and asked his business in the area. Francis replied: 'I am the herald of the Great King. What is it to you?' Their response was to beat him, strip him and search him for valuables. Finding none, they threw him into the snowy ditch and left him for dead.

Strangely exhilarated by the experience, Francis continued on, coming to the Monastery of Santa Maria in Valfabbrica where he asked for help. Known for its charity, the monks at the monastery offered little comfort and no warm clothes. Even worse, Francis was required to work for some thin soup without bread. Years later he met the abbot of the monastery, who remembered the incident and apologized with great shame.

The treasure of the tiny medieval quarter of Valfabbrica is the 12th-century church of Pieve Santa Maria with its frescoes, perhaps painted by the famous artist Cimabue in the 14th century. Valfabbrica was founded around the prominent Monastery of Santa Maria, established by the monks of Nonantola. Today, farming and light industry form its economic base.

Enthusiastically hosting pilgrims, Camere Villa Verde (Via Roma 26, tel 075 9029013, info@camerevillaverde.it) is a small and charming hotel in the heart of town. Also convenient is Ostello Francescano (Via Piave 3, tel 075 901195, info@ostellofrancescano.com, €25/45, €35 with half-board). The local parish, Parrocchia di Santa Maria Assunta (Via Mameli 20, tel 075 901155, valfabbrica@diocesiassisi.it) also has beds available for pilgrims.

STAGE 15
Valfabbrica to Assisi

Start	Main piazza, Valfabbrica
Finish	Basilica di San Francesco, Assisi
Distance	13.4km
Total ascent	530m
Total descent	456m
Difficulty	Easy
Duration	3hrs 45mins
Note	No services are available between Valfabbrica and Assisi, so bring a snack.

Ending at one of the best-loved towns in Italy, this short stage travels among farms and then up into forests as it crosses a ridge to make its way to the hometown of St Francis. Perhaps the most challenging portion is the steep climb in the last 1km before town. Start early so you have more time to enjoy Assisi and its many spiritual and scenic delights.

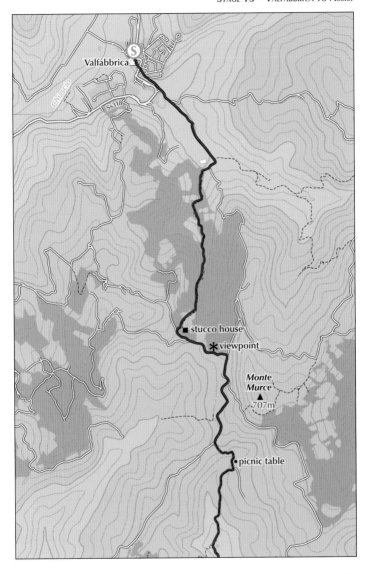

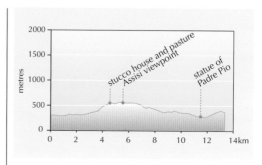

With the piazza and clock tower of Valfabbrica in front of you go left and at the first street, Via Castellana, turn right. The road at first goes downhill then 100m later turns uphill briefly on its way out of town. In another 100m cross Via Roma and continue upward as the road now becomes Via Osteria, which goes up a rise before it descends to the valley floor below. ◄ The houses now become more spread out and you see the high ridge ahead that you will cross.

Enjoy the artful spray-painted graffiti of the life of St Francis on the left as the road descends.

Continue on this quiet lane until you pass between two closely spaced commercial buildings that seem rather out of place in this bucolic setting. Cross a bridge and follow the road uphill and to the right. In 200m turn right onto a gravel road and in 100m pass a bench and fountain for pilgrims. At a fork in 200m go left instead of crossing the creek at a fork to the right, and then begin gradually to gain elevation.

In 300m the road begins to climb more steeply. Turn left at a rusted metal gate as the new, well-graded and wide path of pink gravel gently rises through woods. In 850m the path, now a road, begins to climb more steeply. Just before the summit you come to a bench and then a meadow. The road starts to level out at the **stucco house and pasture** (4.5km) following a climb of about 1km.

Soon you come to a summit at a T-junction. Turn left, going downhill. Just afterward you can see the first glimpse of the Rocco Maggiore fortress and the bare and rounded top of Mount Subasio, the lower slopes of which

are home to Assisi. The road continues uphill and soon after a house you come to **viewpoint** with a wooden cross atop a cairn of stones left by pilgrims. Look south toward the mountain and for the first time see the Basilica of San Francesco, resting place of St Francis, in the distance.

Assisi from the north, with Rocca Maggiore on the left, the Basilica of St Francis on the right

Continue on and turn right on the asphalt road. ▶ Continue downhill for 1.4km and see views to the distant right of the valley between Assisi and Perugia where the Tiber and Chiascio Rivers have their confluence. Just before a grouping of farm buildings, turn left onto a gravel road going downhill, sometimes steeply.

To the left is a picnic table and fountain.

At the bottom of the hill, cross a small creek and begin to climb. In 150m there is a summit with **benches and a picnic table** for a rest. Afterward, at a T-junction, turn right and continue downhill on this gravel road through pine forests and past a derelict house. In 1.2km cross a creek running over the road; the gravel road turns to asphalt in 900m, at a driveway for an agriturismo.

Stay on this asphalt road, which soon is called Via Padre Pio; after 1.3km it ends at a **Statue of Padre Pio** (11.3km) at the bottom of the hill. Turn left on this quiet

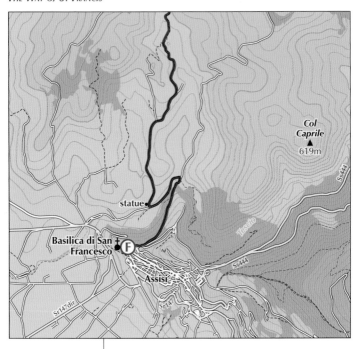

arterial road at the base of Mount Subasio and continue around a hairpin turn. Take the right fork and go past Osteria del Molino and then follow the paving stones over a three-arch bridge, passing a small church. This narrow road with cars coming downhill climbs steeply, covering the 114m rise in just 1.2km.

After a parking lot come to the Porta San Giacomo gate in the city walls. At the gate turn right and walk 400m downhill to the **Basilica di San Francesco**. If you would like to make an application for a testimonium certificate that documents your completion, go to the lower piazza, down the steps from the main level, and speak to the friar at the entry to the cloister, to the left of the lower basilica entry. Ask for the Statio Peregrinorum (pilgrim office). ◄

Note that there is a daily mass at 6.00pm for pilgrims in the lower basilica.

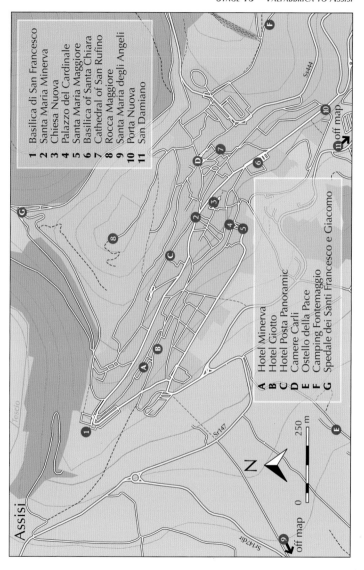

Assisi

1 Basilica di San Francesco
2 Santa Maria Minerva
3 Chiesa Nuova
4 Palazzo del Cardinale
5 Santa Maria Maggiore
6 Basilica of Santa Chiara
7 Cathedral of San Rufino
8 Rocca Maggiore
9 Santa Maria degli Angeli
10 Porta Nuova
11 San Damiano

A Hotel Minerva
B Hotel Giotto
C Hotel Posta Panoramic
D Camere Carli
E Ostello della Pace
F Camping Fontemaggio
G Spedale dei Santi Francesco e Giacomo

Basilica di San Francesco and upper piazza

ASSISI 683M POP 27,683

Even nearly 800 years after his death, the town of Assisi is steeped in the spirit of its most prominent and most humble resident. For the last decades its wise city fathers and mothers, knowing its importance as a pilgrim and tourism destination, have carefully preserved the town's medieval character. The result is a warm and scenic, if perhaps kitschy, taste of medieval life.

To tour Assisi's main sites, begin with its most prominent and iconic building, the Basilica di San Francesco (1). The church, begun just two years after Francis' death, is situated on a rocky projection from Mount Subasio, affording it dramatic views of the Spoleto Valley and assuring it can be seen for many miles around. The oldest part of the basilica is the lower, Romanesque level, which contains the tomb of St Francis, along with those of his four closest friends – Rufino, Leone, Masseo and Angelo. His patroness, Lady Jacoba (or Brother Jacoba as he lovingly called her) is buried at the entrance stairway to this level, facing the altar. To the right of the main altar and down some stairs is the Chapel of the Relics, which contains the sandals and tunic of Francis, among other historic items. In the upper basilica is a high altar, directly over Francis' tomb. Frescoes by Giotto, Cimabue, Cavallini and others adorn the walls of the early Gothic-style nave. While these cherished artworks were damaged in the earthquake of 1997, their careful restoration allows them still to tell the story of Francis' life. The entire basilica is well worth a long and meditative visit. Continue the tour by walking out

Santa Maria Minerva and the Torre Comune at Piazza Comune

the main door of the basilica's upper level to the Upper Piazza of San Francesco, then follow the road straight ahead, the Via San Francesco, which becomes the Via Fortini and Via Portica before arriving at the Piazza del Comune. In the piazza is Santa Maria Minerva (2) with its ancient, Roman columns. Here Francis and his friends first opened the Bible and found the call to poverty. Little but the ancient columns remain from the church of Francis' day.

Back in the piazza make a hard right before the fountain to see the Chiesa Nuova (3), built over the traditional site of Francis' parents' home, where his father imprisoned Francis after his well-intentioned theft of precious cloth.

Downhill, past the church of San Antonio is Santa Maria Maggiore (4), which was the cathedral church of Assisi until the 11th century. This is the site of the trial by the bishop in which Francis renounced his parents and returned his clothes to them. In this square note the fountain, old enough to have been witness to this event. From the door of the church, turn right and follow Via Santa Agnese past the Palazzo del Cardinale (11), home to Francis' friend and protector, Bishop Guido.

Now turn toward the right and come to the spacious Piazza Santa Chiara and the grand Basilica di Santa Chiara (5), built on the site of San Giorgio, where Clare first heard her friend Francis preach. Inspired by his example, Clare founded the Order of the Poor Clares, and became a holy woman in her own right, revered by bishops and popes. Her body is kept in the crypt downstairs, along with relics that include her hair, a breviary of Francis, and many other articles from her life. The cross that spoke to Francis at San Damiano is now in a small chapel to the right of the altar on the main floor.

After touring the church, turn right from the front doors and walk around the building, through the archways and along Via Santa Chiara. After the Porta Nuova

(10) you can turn right and follow the steps and narrow road steeply downhill to San Damiano (6). Although it is a fair walk down (and back up), this church is filled with history. Here Francis heard the words, 'Rebuild my church,' and devoted himself to rebuilding the crumbling structure, not realizing his life would help rebuild the entire Church of his day. Here also Clare was cloistered with her disciples, and here St Francis completed his immortal *Canticle of Brother Sun*.

If you have time, a visit to San Rufino (7), Assisi's Cathedral and site of the baptisms of Francis and Clare, is in order. While in the upper part of town it is also worthwhile to tour the Rocca Maggiore castle (8), which dominates the town. A very pleasant couple of hours can be spent walking down the brick-lined path to Santa Maria degli Angeli (9) on the valley floor below town. At the transept crossing inside this grand, baroque church is the Porziuncola – a church within a church. This tiny chapel is the place where Francis began his order and where, surrounded by his devoted followers, he breathed his last breath. Buses leave every few minutes for the return trip above to Assisi; or simply walk uphill for 30mins along the brick sidewalk and enjoy the excellent views of Assisi and the Basilica di San Francesco.

Assisi has several lower-cost hotels, including the convenient Hotel Minerva (A) (Piazzetta R Bonghi 7, tel 075 812416, info@hotelminervaassisi.com, €50/75). Also convenient are Hotel Posta Panoramic (B) (Via San Paolo 11, tel 075 812558, info@hotelpostaassisi.it, €51/81 includes breakfast) and Camere Carli (C) (Piazza San Rufino, tel 075 812490, info@camerecarli.it, €37/47, no breakfast), in a quiet and sunny part of town. If you are in the mood to splurge, one of many more expensive choices is the posh, historic and picturesque Hotel Giotto (D) (Via Fontebella 41, tel 075 812209, info@hotelgiottoassisi.it, from €115). Situated just south and below town is Ostello della Pace (E) (Via di Valecchie 177, tel 075 816767, from €18 including breakfast). Located 800m outside Porta Cappuccini is Camping Fontemaggio (F) (Via Eremo Carceri 24, tel 075 812317, info@fontemaggio.it), which as well as camping has a youth hostel on-site (€22, plus €6 breakfast) plus a hotel of its own (€35/54, €4 breakfast). Assisi's pilgrim stewards are justifiably proud of their new pilgrim-only hostel (G), the Speddale Francesco e Giacomo (Via degli Episcopi, north of the walled city, near the city's Cimitero Monumentale, 15 beds, contact information not available at the time of writing) with its flavour of the Camino de Santiago.

3 ASSISI TO RIETI

Sunrise over scenic Poggio Bustone (Stage 23)

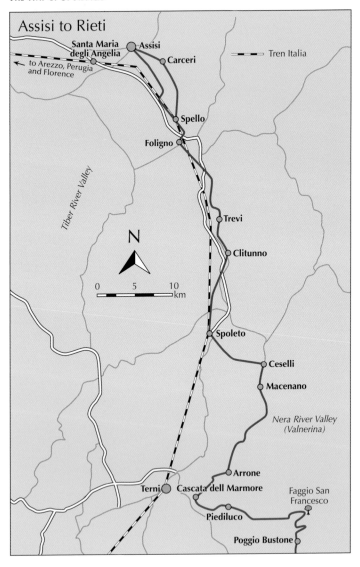

Assisi to Rieti

Santa Maria degli Angelia — Assisi
Carceri
to Arezzo, Perugia and Florence
- - - Tren Italia
Spello
Foligno

Tiber River Valley

N

0   5   10
km

Trevi

Clitunno

Spoleto

Ceselli

Macenano

Nera River Valley (Valnerina)

Arrone
Cascata dell Marmore   Faggio San Francesco
Terni
Piediluco
Poggio Bustone

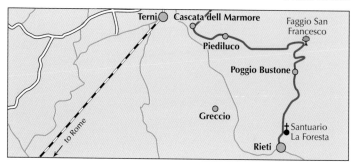

Beginning in Assisi and ending 136km later in Rieti, the pathways of this part of the Way of St Francis hug steep mountainsides, giving panoramic views of the fertile valleys below. The first days are spent walking through olive groves while nights are spent in historic hill towns like Spello, Trevi and Spoleto.

The municipalities' varied and charming medieval character makes each compete for the most favored place in the pilgrim's heart. Spello lures tourists looking for a living, working medieval town with cafés and gift shops. Lofty Trevi, off the tourist track, is quieter, without the flocks of sightseers but with even more charismatic allure. Spoleto is renown for its culture and sophistication, and attracts music lovers from around the world to its annual Due Mondi festival.

After Spoleto, the route ascends Monte Luco and climbs along the slopes of Monte Piano before descending to the quiet Nera River Valley with its protected forests and recreational nature trails. After enjoying pleasant walks along the Nera, pilgrims are treated to the majestic waterfall at Cascata delle Marmore, a wonder of the Roman Empire. And if that does not contain enough awe and wonder, a walk up into the foothills below Monte Terminillo brings you to a remote and beautiful experience of unspoilt natural beauty where you can touch a 1000-year-old beech tree, Faggio San Francesco, said to have been blessed by the saint himself.

Even 800 years later the area is infused with the presence of the humble saint and his followers. The Franciscan convent at Monteluco, the cave of his spiritual transformation at Poggio Bustone, and his beloved La Foresta are Franciscan touchstones along the way. When this part ends at Rieti – largest town on the trek between Florence and Rome – there is still more of Francis to explore nearby. Pilgrims can take extra time and visit Greccio and Fonte Colombo, cherished sites waiting to tell their own stories of Francis and his love of God and all God's creatures.

153

STAGE 16
Assisi to Spello (easier route)

Start	Basilica di San Francesco, Assisi
Finish	Upper gate, Spello
Distance	13.8km
Total ascent	301m
Total descent	429m
Difficulty	Easy
Duration	3hrs 30mins
Note	While less scenic than the more difficult route up Mount Subasio, this itinerary offers a quick walk to Spello among olive groves with wide views of the valley floor below.

The lower route of the two options for today leads gently through olive orchards toward scenic and touristic Spello, allowing plenty of time to enjoy the shops and restaurants of this justifiably popular Umbrian hill town.

A left at this fork takes you uphill on the more strenuous option that climbs partway up Mount Subasio; for directions see Stage 16A.

With the front door of the Basilica di San Francesco behind you go straight ahead, following the right-hand walkway toward the Via San Francesco. Continue on this street gently uphill to the main Piazza del Comune, and at the fountain ahead go right and slightly downhill. ◄

Continue along what is now Corso Giuseppe Mazzini and pass the piazza in front of Basilica di Santa Chiara with its wide view over the valley. Continue through a second gate along Borgo Arentino to a third and final gate – Porta Nuova. Go straight along the road and come to the bottom of a 'U' curve with a parking lot on the right. Take the fork to the right and then go straight at the traffic circle, which puts you briefly on Via della Madonna dell'Olivo.

At a small shrine to the Virgin Mary, turn left and go uphill on **Via San Benedetto**; views of the valley and Santa Maria degli Angeli now open up to the right.

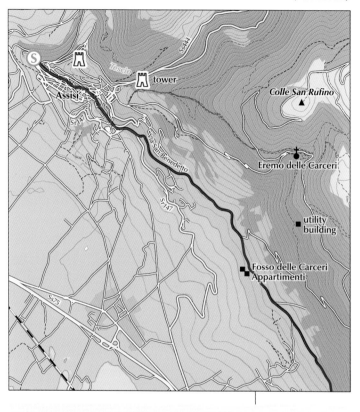

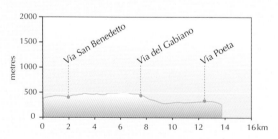

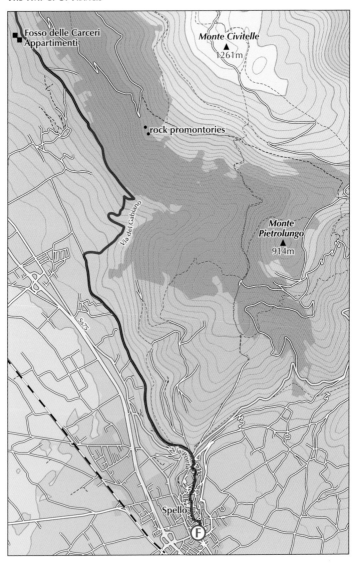

Fosso delle Carceri
Appartimenti

Monte Civitelle
1261m

rock promontories

Via del Gabbiano

*Monte
Pietrolungo*
914m

SS75

Via Poeta

Spello

F

The Porta Nuova in Assisi

After the small Convento Elisabettina di Padova on the right take the fork to the left, going uphill. Now the road becomes more pastoral, with olive trees on the right and gardens and orchards on the left.

After the **Fosso delle Carceri Appartimenti** take the middle of three forks, going straight ahead. Here the road becomes more level and the asphalt becomes patchy and broken. Stay on the asphalt at the next fork, then at the intersection with the asphalt road 450m later go right and downhill.

In 600m is another triple fork. Take the middle fork again, toward Agriturismo Le Madrile di San Paolo. The Parco di Monte Subasio is now on the left side and soon its forests will adjoin you on the left. In 650m go downhill and right onto an asphalt road that soon becomes gravel. Continue on this road for the next 2.3km until the **Via del Gabiano**. Turn right here and 200m later, at an unmarked brown gravel road, turn left into the olive orchards.

This gravel road zigzags its way downhill until 500m later it is joined on the right by the gravel offshoot of an abandoned asphalt road. Continue straight, walking

Spello seen from Via Poeta

between a house and its garage onto a two-track gravel road.

In a hairpin turn 300m later go right and immediately veer left, passing a house and garden and two derelict stone houses. The gravel road ends in 200m. Go right and 600m later this road ends at a larger asphalt road. Turn left. At an unmarked intersection in 200m go left and continue on this road – aptly named Via degli Olivi – for 3km until it ends at **Via Poeta**, the road into Spello. Turn left and continue uphill. The street is now lined with tall trees, with a stone wall on the left and beautiful views of pretty Spello on the right. Just before the first archway the alternate route from Assisi joins from the left.

For information about Spello, including accommodation listings, see the conclusion of Stage 16A.

STAGE 16A

Assisi to Spello (harder route)

Start	Basilica di San Francesco, Assisi
Finish	Piazza J F Kennedy, Spello
Distance	17.6km
Total ascent	925m
Total descent	1024m
Difficulty	Hard
Duration	5hrs 30mins
Note	Plan to leave early so that you can be at Eremo delle Carceri before 9.00am, when the tourist vans begin to fill this otherwise quiet, meditative place with outside noise.

This challenging climb offers truly spectacular views of the Tiber Valley, plus an opportunity to turn off the trail and see Eremo delle Carceri. Longer by only 2km than the easier route, the extra elevation gain of 500m in the first 5km makes it a challenging walk.

Starting at the Basilica di San Francesco, walk along Via San Francesco to Piazza del Comune. After the fountain, go left onto the sidewalk, following the blue-and-yellow sign that reads, 'Spello – Cammino Escursionistico EE,

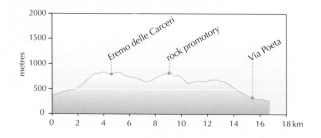

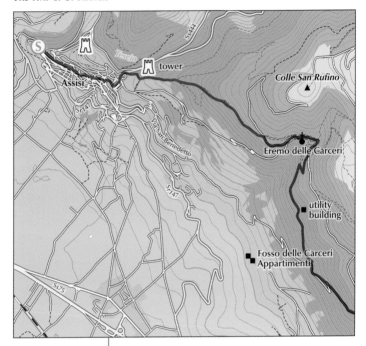

Cammino Difficile.' After a short uphill walk you reach Piazza San Rufino.

Take the driveway to the left of the cathedral building, go through the arch and walk uphill. In 200m is Piazza Matteotti, which is bisected by a wide auto road. Turn left on the road, enjoying views of the castle Rocca Maggiore on the left, and then walk straight ahead through the upper city gate. With the beautiful panoramas of the forests of Bosco San Francesco and the surrounding mountains on the left, turn right onto a path just after the gate. The day's first climb now begins.

In just 100m is an unmarked fork in the path; go right onto the smaller path that leads steeply uphill and toward the **Rocca Minore tower** that was the uppermost defense of medieval Assisi. At the tower, turn left and walk uphill on the often very steep gravel road. In 500m you come to a triple fork; take the middle fork, leading to Eremo delle Carceri. A pause in the climb comes in about 800m where CAI 53 branches off. Stay on CAI 50 toward Eremo delle Carceri, which goes straight, traversing the side of the mountain.

The path continues its climb, and recent construction of an underground pipeline has kept the track wide and well-graded as it gains elevation. In 700m pass a stone hut that serves the waterworks and 100m later come to a picnic area. Just 20m after the picnic area turn right on the asphalt road going downhill. After 500m you come to the turn-off for **Eremo delle Carceri**, with its front gate 100m below, with a small bar and gift kiosk, as well as the hermitage itself.

> Originally a series of prison cells used by the town of Assisi and afterwards a Benedictine monastery, **Carceri** ('prison' in Italian) became an important retreat for Francis and his disciples. The nearby caves provided modest shelter, and the quiet pathways of Mount Subasio offered beauty and solitude.
>
> The tiny Franciscan convent here consists of 15th-century buildings completed by St Bernardino of Siena, but the innermost chapel dates back to the time of Francis. It is said that, commanded by Francis, water first gushed from the well that is in the center of the tiny convent.
>
> The entire area has a calm and quiet aura, and it is easy to see how it could have been a place of meditation for Francis and his brothers. (With advance permission Eremo delle Carceri has basic accommodation available for people who wish to remain for retreats. See **www.eremodellecarceri.it**.)

After your visit, retrace your steps up to the main road and continue on it uphill as it winds around the back of the hermitage. A stone wall marks the right side of the road, and when the stone wall ends take an earthen path off the road going downhill and to the right. In 350m the path ends at a T-junction with CAI 54. Turn right, going downhill, and in 150m arrive at the locked rear gate of the hermitage grounds.

Continue on the path and in 200m come to a meadow with a large stone **utility building** and a small shrine on the left. Now the path becomes a wide gravel drive. In 150m go left at the fork and soon come to a small stone house with a red roof. In 900m, switchbacks take you downhill to an asphalt road. Turn left on the road, in the direction of a sign that reads, 'Monastero Benedetto di Monte Subasio.'

In 700m turn left off the asphalt road onto a narrow shortcut trail. Follow this path for 350m until it returns to the road. At the road, turn left, going uphill and continue on the road for 1.1km as it climbs to a hairpin curve. At the curve be careful not to miss the path as it goes straight ahead instead of turning with the road. Note the sign that reads 'CAI 01' and 'Spello 2.15h.'

Eremo delle Carceri, beloved by Francis for its quiet

Soon comes one of the most memorable places on this entire journey: on the left in 250m is a **rock promontory** with a breathtaking view for anyone brave enough

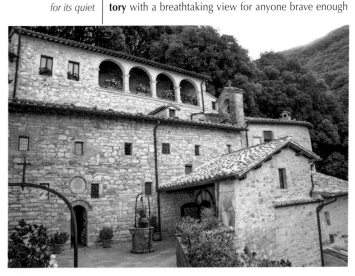

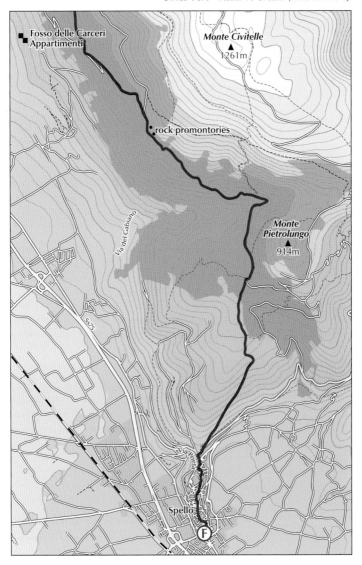

Wide view of the Tiber Valley from a rock promontory on the upper path

to scramble up its steep face. On a sheer embankment about 600m above the valley, the granite outcropping overlooks a vast stretch of the Tiber Valley, with everything visible from Perugia and Assisi to the north, to Trevi and the lower parts of Spoleto to the south. Take some extra time to contemplate life and the special joy of experiencing a sight that is accessible only to those able and willing to make such a tiring and difficult climb.

But wait: continue along the path another 150m and come to a second outcropping at about the same elevation with an equally incredible view that does not require mountain-goat abilities to enjoy. This second outcropping is an even better place to pause and enjoy the splendor of a sweeping view over the valley, hundreds of meters below.

Continue along the path, coming to a fork with CAI 54. Stay on CAI 56 and in 300m come to a fork where you turn left. Soon you begin a downhill track and in 800m take a left at an easy-to-miss fork. Just 200m later the narrow trail you have been on ends at a wide gravel road. Turn left here, going uphill, and then in 700m turn right at the fork, going downhill toward Spello.

In about 100m you come to the southern boundary of Mount Subasio Park and are on a nicely graded, 2m-wide pathway under trees. Continue on this road for the next 1.4km until it starts a downhill trajectory toward Spello. Now wide panoramas open up facing tomorrow's itinerary – Foligno, on the valley floor, and beautiful Trevi, on the mountain slope to the left. Continue straight ahead onto a now narrower path leading downhill toward olive groves. At an intersection in 100m turn right and follow this road, going straight through a triple intersection in 30m, as the road leads downhill.

Very soon you catch your first glimpses of the rooftops of Spello straight ahead. The gravel road turns to asphalt in 700m and in another 500m you come to a smooth asphalt road. Turn right to get into Spello. At a T-junction in 200m turn left onto **Viale Poeta** where those who have taken the easier path from Assisi also enter Spello.

Enter the town and walk through the Piazza Valle Gloria, then veer left through another arch and downhill past Fratello Sole B&B on the right and then Cacciatore Trattoria e Albergo on the left. Turn left at the small piazza just afterward and go downhill, and in 100m come to the tree-lined central piazza of **Spello** with its town hall, restaurants, bank and grocery store.

Looking down to Spello

Continue downhill past Chiesa di Sant'Andrea and Santa Maria Maggiore, two of Spello's twenty-seven medieval or Renaissance churches. Turn left at Capella Di Sant'Anna onto Via Consolare and follow it to the tower and arch, leading to the lowest of the town's historic squares, Piazza J F Kennedy.

SPELLO 280M POP 8585

From the valley below, Spello typifies the scenic Italian hill town – built on the slopes of a mountain to afford protection from roving bands of brigands. Up close, Spello is unusually well tended, charming and vibrant.

Perhaps because of its annual Infiorate Festival – when the streets of the old city are elaborately decorated with intricate carpets of flower petals – Spello has captured the attention of those looking for a slice of historic Italian village life. The flower festival, held for over 150 years, is observed annually on the day of Corpus Domini, the ninth Sunday after Easter. Locals spend days planning and creating complicated designs, while visitors throng the streets to admire them. Afterward the designs pave the way for the Procession of Corpus Christi, led by the bishop, atop the brilliant and colorful mile-long path.

Spello is an ancient town, founded by the Umbrians, and later called Hispellum by the Romans. Ruins of a Roman amphitheater lay on the north side of town. After its flower festival, Spello is perhaps best known for the nearly two-dozen medieval churches within its walls. Among the several 11th- and 12th-century churches, Santa Maria Maggiore, with its frescoes by Perugino and Pinturicchio, is particularly noteworthy.

Although the churches have stood many centuries, older by over a millennium is the town's Porta di Venere, which dates from the first century BC, and the Porta Consolare just a few centuries newer.

Inside the walls and with a remarkable view toward Trevi are Albergo Il Cacciatore (Via Giulia 42, tel 0742 301603, info@ilcacciatorehotel.com, with a pilgrim price of €75 for a double room) and Fratello Sole B&B (tel 0742 651902, bebfratellosole@libero.it, €50/75). Less expensive but just outside the city walls are Nuovo Albergo il Portonaccio (tel 0742 651313, info@albergoilportonaccio.it, €40/49) and Hotel del Prato Paolucci (Via Brodolini 4, tel 0742 301018, €35/50). The Augustinian sisters at Convento Santa Maria Maddalena have pilgrim beds available (tel 0742 301285, agostinianespello@alice.it), as does the Convento Piccolo San Damiano (tel 0742 651182).

STAGE 17
Spello to Trevi

Start	J F Kennedy Piazza, Spello
Finish	Main (nuova) piazza, Trevi
Distance	19.1km
Total ascent	429m
Total descent	243m
Difficulty	Moderate
Duration	5hrs 30mins
Note	An intermediate stop at Foligno offers several options for a late breakfast or early lunch.

The stage begins among quiet farms at the valley floor, leading through modern suburbs to delightful downtown Foligno. After another suburban trek the road rises through rolling hills covered in olive orchards to the picturesque and unspoiled hill town of Trevi.

Standing in the Piazza J F Kennedy in the lower portion of the old city of Spello, face the ancient Porta Consolare and pass on its right side. Follow Via Sant'Anna outside of the city walls on unusual brown aggregate pavement and go right at the fork onto Via Brodolini. You now leave the picturesque old city behind you and follow this road 1.4km along farms and fields through several intersections as it becomes Via Spineto and then takes a sweeping right turn, pointing toward Foligno.

In 1.4km you come to an intersection with a large road. Now in the outskirts of Foligno, go straight ahead through this and a second intersection toward a residential area. At the end of the road is Auto Strada SS75 (3.4km). Cross the freeway in the underpass and turn left onto a patchy asphalt road. Follow the road along the freeway for 200m and then turn right, away from the freeway onto a narrow asphalt road between homes. Watch for speeding cars here and enjoy the pilgrim shrine on the right.

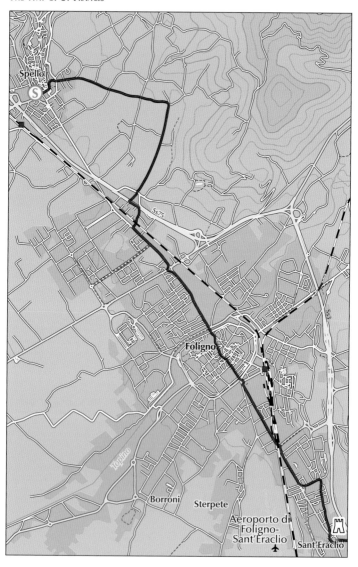

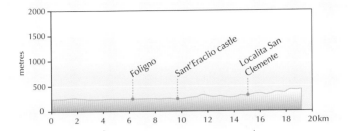

In 200m cross the train tracks and 100m later turn left onto the sidewalk along the busy Viale Firenze. Continue on the sidewalk and go through the right side of a traffic circle in 600m. The street is now lined with trees and leads on a gradual downhill slope in 1.1km to the **Topino River**.

Cross the bridge into the historic center of **Foligno**, following grey paving stones to the right at the fork along Via XX Settembre to the archway in 500m that leads to the charming Piazza delle Repubblica with its café/ bars, banks, gelato shops and impressive 12th-century Cattedrale di San Feliciano (6.2km).

FOLIGNO 234M POP 56,688

Although about 80 per cent of Foligno was destroyed by Allied bombardment during World War II, the town has heroically recreated its historic center, ensuring that its urban heart retained its medieval character. On sunny mornings the piazza is filled with local residents enjoying a cup of coffee or strolling among the shops.

The Cattedrale di Santa Feliciano, built in the twelfth century, is dedicated to the bishop and martyr of the second and third centuries who evangelized in the area. Two blocks south of the piazza is the Church of San Francesco and its tomb of Blessed Angela of Foligno (1248–1309), a Franciscan mystic known for her ecstatic visions and meticulous attention to Francis' way of poverty.

Right on the river before the central city is Hotel Le Mura (Via Mentata 25, tel 0742 357344, info@lemura.net, €60/95). Also available and much less expensive is Ostello di Foligno (Via Pierantoni 21, tel 0742 353776, info@ostellodifoligno. it, €30/48, dormitory €20), just off Via Garibaldi, a few blocks northeast of the cathedral.

Foligno town hall

With the cathedral at your back go straight ahead onto the pedestrian mall Corso Cavour. At the end, carefully cross the busy Viale Battisti in the direction of the pharmacy, going straight ahead onto Viale Roma. Continue past a military complex behind a high stone wall on this tree-lined street, past the railway yard and uphill to a traffic circle. Go around the traffic circle on the left side and continue 500m to a second traffic circle. Now visible on the mountain ahead is Trevi, goal for the day.

At this traffic circle abandon the Viale Roma and turn left, going up toward the hills on a two-lane road. Turn right at the next street, Via Flaminia Vecchia, and follow it

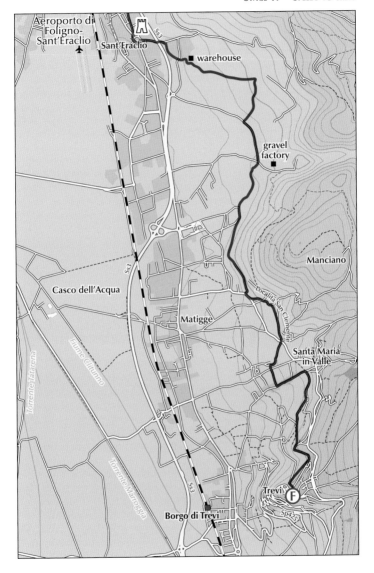

through a quiet neighborhood of two-story homes in the suburban town of Sant'Eraclio. In 1.5km you come to the archway (9.5km) of the town's small **castle**.

Go on the narrow street through the archway, pass a butcher shop, and come out the other gate of the castle. Now turn left onto the Via della Collina and follow it uphill past a bar and pizzeria, the last services available until Trevi. Continue on this road under the Auto Strada Statale SS3 and one block later turn right on Via Londra.

Follow this road through a three-way intersection, walking toward a **warehouse** building painted with a bear and dragonflies. Turn right just before this building, still on Via Londra, and follow as it turns 90 degrees left. After the upcoming driveway take the next fork on asphalt to the right, as Via Londra continues uphill on gravel to the left.

In 300m this road turns to gravel. Go straight ahead, with olive orchards on the right. At a small sign veer right, then at the next fork go left. Soon you come to an intersection of three roads. Take the half-right road, enjoying views of the wide valley below. The road continues through olive orchards and after a time curves right, goes downhill and then passes a brick-and-stucco building. It then comes to an intersection overlooking a **gravel factory**. Turn left here onto the narrow asphalt road by the white building with an arch and then veer right at the next intersection.

Continue through olive groves, crossing Via Vocabolo Formoni, then take the next fork to the left. Go straight at the following intersection and soon afterwards leave the olive orchards behind and head up into the woods above the olive groves. After a green chain link fence you enter a narrow, single-track path on gravel going through the woods.

In 300m the gravel path ends at an asphalt road. Turn uphill, to the left, onto Via San Nicolo, and go left at the fork after a grouping of houses. Continue until the road itself turns right and then comes to an asphalt road 50m later. Turn left on the asphalt road and 100m later turn left again onto the asphalt **Localita San Clemente**, which curves uphill.

At a fork with a tiny utility building in the middle (15.1km) turn right and in 100m turn right again, keeping the yellow stucco wall on your left. The road now turns left. Turn right in front of a stone wall at the next road. In 300m this road is joined by another road from the left; continue straight and in another 300m come to a three-way intersection. Turn right along the first road and then cross the second road and go straight onto a narrow gravel drive, keeping the olive orchards on your left.

Trevi's main, upper piazza and clock tower

MODERN TREVI 412M POP 8176

Modern Trevi is divided into two halves – Upper Trevi above and Borgo Trevi below. While the upper town is virtually unspoiled in its medieval character, Borgo Trevi is somewhat pedestrian in its 20th century, suburban feel. A hilly walk of 3km separates the two.

Trevi is first mentioned in the historical record by Pliny the Elder, who wrote that the Umbrians founded 'Treviae'. The oldest portion of the extant city wall dates to the first century BC and the inner of two walls that surround the old city are of Roman origin. Trevi has 20 old churches, and the Madonna delle Lacrima (15th–16th-century), located 1km south of town, includes frescoes by Perugino – the last signed works of the 16th-century master.

The best way to enjoy Trevi is to walk its quiet streets, enjoy a coffee or glass of wine in the bar of a piazza, and catch views of the valley below from the heights of its ancient walls. Trevi's gift is the simple joy of spending an afternoon surrounded by a town that still looks and feels much as it did hundreds of years ago.

Owners of the lovely Antica Dimora alla Rocca hotel (tel 0742 38541, info@hotelal-larocca.it, from €65) in the old city have reserved one multi-bed room under the eaves for pilgrims. On the west slope of the city, the Monastero di Santa Chiara (tel 0742 78216, monasterosantachi.es@tiscali.it) and Monastero di Santa Lucia (tel 0742 78242, **www.monasterosantalucia.it**) also make rooms available for pilgrims.

The road becomes asphalt in 400m. Turn left at the next asphalt road through olive groves and then cross another asphalt road going straight ahead toward a small chapel. At a fork in 200m go right and then veer left just before a tidy stone house. Come to a stone wall and turn left, aiming uphill between closely spaced homes on Via Collecchio toward **Santa Maria in Valle**. Pass the Hotel Residence Paradiso and at a new stone wall turn right. Head toward a small shrine and then re-enter the olive orchards where the road turns to gravel and begins going slowly downhill.

Soon the path follows a wooden fence on the right, then a horse pasture and stable. For the next 300m you follow this quiet forest path, which then intersects with an asphalt road. Turn left here and then left again for a scramble up a steep hill on jagged, loose gravel before reaching the Via San Martino. Turn right and follow this road past the church on the left, then a children's play area followed by a war memorial and finally come to the large, lower, main piazza of old **Trevi** with its café/bars and restaurants. ◄

The tourist information is in a palazzo to the left and the winding, picturesque streets of the upper town are to the right.

STAGE 18

Trevi to Spoleto

Start	Main (nuovo) piazza, Trevi
Finish	Spoleto Duomo
Distance	18.8km
Total ascent	275m
Total descent	363m
Difficulty	Easy
Duration	4hrs 30mins
Note	Food and restrooms are available at café/bars in Clitunno (6.4km) and on the San Giacomo option (12km). An early start allows more time to enjoy Spoleto, one of Umbria's most beloved cities.

Some camino guides direct pilgrims through Poreta to reach Spoleto, adding another day to the itinerary. Instead, this route connects to Spoleto on the valley floor, through olive orchards and onto a paved bike path to charming Spoleto in just one day.

Starting at the large, modern piazza of upper Trevi, go to the right of the tourist information office and follow the narrow road downhill between stone walls. At a stop sign in 300m go left, and just afterward veer right at an antique light post and follow this path downhill.

At a second stop sign cross the street and go straight ahead onto the narrow asphalt road that quickly becomes gravel. Soon you come to a wide asphalt road; continue straight (left) onto the road and at an asphalt road in 400m turn right, heading to the ridge and the town of **Bovara** where you can enjoy beautiful views of the valley as well as scenic Trevi behind you.

Just after coming to the Bovara city limit sign go straight at the intersection and then immediately come to a fork. Here there are blue/yellow markers and red/white markers pointing to the left. Instead, follow the yellow

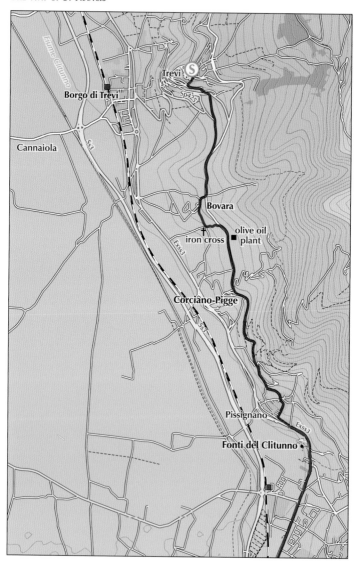

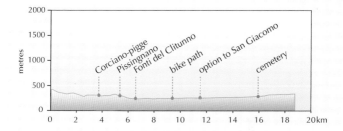

arrows to the right for the shorter way to Spoleto. As you walk down the hill you can see the town of Spoleto straight ahead in the distance.

At the peach-colored house in 300m, follow the road downhill and to the right in the direction of the Spoleto road sign. At the next fork, turn left. Soon the road comes to another fork, with yellow arrows pointing downhill. Instead, turn left in the direction of the café/bar.

In 200m, at the **iron cross**, turn left and go uphill toward an old three-story house. The road veers to the left and then crosses between two homes, spilling out onto the driveway of a grey stucco house. Take the sidewalk and soon find yourself walking uphill on a narrow alley between two chain link fences. Turn right in 100m at the top of the path onto the asphalt road, Via Norcia.

Walk along the road, enjoying the views amid the olive trees. Pass the Frantoio Lucentini **olive oil plant** and in 800m come to the outskirts of **Corciano-Pigge**. A road soon joins from the left and you come to a church with a squarish bell tower. Just after the church watch for a left turn off the road. Take the turn and follow the path to a yellow stucco house. Now turn left onto the narrow asphalt road among olive trees that curves along the shoulder of the mountain toward a castle.

Go straight through the next intersection and then turn right at the fork just after an old bench. In 500m the asphalt road turns to gravel and continues its climb through olive groves. You come in 300m to a high stone wall of the Castello Pissignano (built between the 12th and 15th centuries) and then reach a gathering of homes. The path turns into a concrete sidewalk, which you follow as it zigzags among houses. Turn right at the asphalt road, Via del Castello, and go downhill toward the red-domed church and tower of **Pissignano** (5.3km).

Follow the road to the right of the church and continue straight ahead along Via Franceschini. At the first intersection downhill are signs for alternate walking routes; pass this intersection and at the next intersection turn left at the guardrail just before a yellow apartment building. Stay on the asphalt road as it weaves its way downhill, past gravel driveways toward the valley floor.

In 300m the road ends at a T-junction with Via Flaminia. Turn left and very soon you come to the Green Garden Bar, a good place to rest. Cross the road toward the green and peaceful **Fonti del Clitunno** park and its spring-fed canals, featuring swans, a bar, a gelateria, and, finally, a trattoria. At the trattoria pick up a small asphalt walkway and follow it 350m to an agriturismo where it spills out onto the wide shoulder of the highway. Go straight ahead on the wide shoulder of Viale Settecamini until Il Camminetto Ristorante, where a **bike path** commences on the left side of the road.

The pond and manicured lawns of Fonti del Clitunno

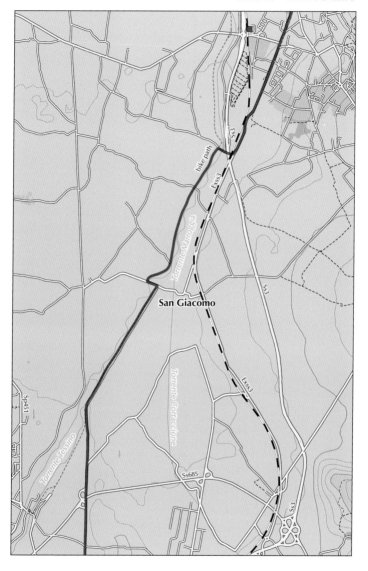

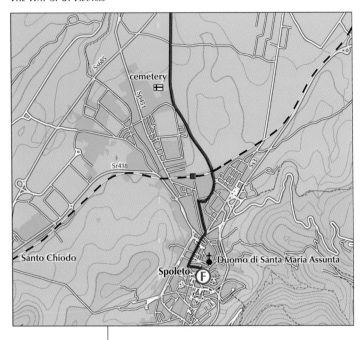

Continue until the bike path ends, then carefully follow the shoulder of the highway toward the Strada Statale Flaminia bridge. Just before the bridge, follow a right-turn lane in the direction of Assano and turn right off the highway. Cross the railroad tracks, then cross under the bridge and 200m later turn left onto the Assisi–Spoleto **bike path** (9.3km).

Continue along the quiet bike path for the next 2.2km until it ends at a bridge. Cross the bridge, going left, and 200m later turn back onto the bike path. ◄ The bike path comes to a bridge in 2km. Turn off the bike path here and get onto the narrow road to the left. Carefully follow this road straight and cross under the Tre Valli Umbre highway bridge, enjoying views of Spoleto ahead. Pass a **cemetery** in 1.2km and continue into the city limits of Spoleto.

Instead of turning here you have the option to go straight ahead into **San Giacomo** for services.

View from Corso Garibaldi, leading upward to the Duomo and Rocca Albornoziana fortress above

At the traffic circle veer left onto Via Caduti di Nassirya. Cross the railroad bridge in 1.7km and stay right at the next traffic circle. The road now curves downhill and to the right. Turn left onto Viale Trento e Trieste after a tangerine-colored apartment building. ▶

The Spoleto Stazione (train station) is three blocks to the right from here.

Head uphill along the shops of this newer part of town, passing a laundromat and supermarket. Cross to the right side of the street and at the next traffic circle veer to the right on Via Flaminia. Pass through the archway into the beautiful Centro Storico of **Spoleto**, onto its main pedestrian street, Corso Garibaldi, with its charming shops and restaurants.

To reach the cathedral through Spoleto's serpentine streets and alleys, follow Corso Garibaldi right and uphill, then turn left onto Via Elladio, right onto Via Salara Vecchia and left onto Via del Duomo. Turn right onto Via Fontesecca and then a slight left onto Via Saffi. After a left onto Via del Duomo you come finally to the Piazza del Duomo and the **Duomo di Santa Maria Assunta**.

SPOLETO 396M POP 38,283

The Duomo's jewel-toned apse frescoes

Situated at a strategic entry to the Tiber River Valley, the city of Spoleto has ancient roots, tracing its beginnings to the Umbrian people of pre-Roman times. Spoletium, as the Romans called it, is mentioned many times in ancient Roman literature, and its Roman amphitheater, today largely restored, is testament to the prosperity and importance of the town in that period.

In addition to the amphitheater, Spoleto is rich in architectural treasures. Its Basilica of San Salvatore, which dates from the late fourth century, is a UNESCO World Heritage site and an important example of early basilica-style church architecture.

The Duomo of Santa Maria Assunta, which dates from the 12th century, contains the tomb of the 15th-century painter Filippo Lippi, who painted the beautiful, jewel-toned scenes from the life of the Virgin Mary in the ceiling of church's 12th-century apse. The church's Romanesque facade and tower exude a gentle and warm presence over the Duomo's piazza. One of its most prized treasures, though, is an original, signed letter of St Francis to Brother Leo. One of only two extant signatures by the saint, the letter can be viewed in the Reliquary Chapel off the left aisle.

Looming over the town is the immense 15th-century Rocca Albornoziana fortress. The fortress now serves as a museum and a series of escalators from the lower part of town allow easy pedestrian access.

The impressive Ponte delle Torri aqueduct spans a deep gorge, standing on huge towers since its construction in the 13th century. Now used solely as a pedestrian bridge, the enormous structure connects Spoleto to Monteluco to the south and serves as the beginning of tomorrow's stage over the mountain to Ceselli.Spoleto's world-famous Due Mondi festival attracts classical virtuosi from Europe and the US each June to early July to perform in its public places and enjoy the town's classic charm.

Given its status as a cultural center, Spoleto has many fine and expensive hotels. Among the less expensive options are Hotel Athena (Via Valadier 3, tel 0743 224218, atherna_hotel@hotmail.com, €35/45) and Hotel Aurora (Via dell'Apollinare 3, tel 0743 220315, info@hotelauroraspoleto.it, €30/40). Although there is no hostel in town, the Instituto Suore Bambin Gesu (Via Castello 4, tel 0733 638309, suore@bambingesu.org) offers single, double and triple rooms for pilgrims.

STAGE 19
Spoleto to Ceselli

Start	Piazza dei Duomo, Spoleto
Finish	Ceselli Community Center
Distance	15.3km
Total ascent	641m
Total descent	663m
Difficulty	Hard
Duration	6hrs 30mins
Note	If you choose to end your day in the tiny settlement of Ceselli, plan to bring food for both lunch and dinner since there is no store or restaurant available. Alternately, continue another 5.1km on easy paths to Macenano's hotel and restaurant along tomorrow's itinerary.

After a very steep first hour to the Franciscan convent of Monteluco, this stage crosses a vast forest, traversing mountainsides along paths that offer breathtaking views of the Tiber and Nera River Valleys and mountains beyond. After a steep downhill path, followed by a long and quiet asphalt road, the stage ends at the tiny settlement of Ceselli and its solitary agriturismo accommodation.

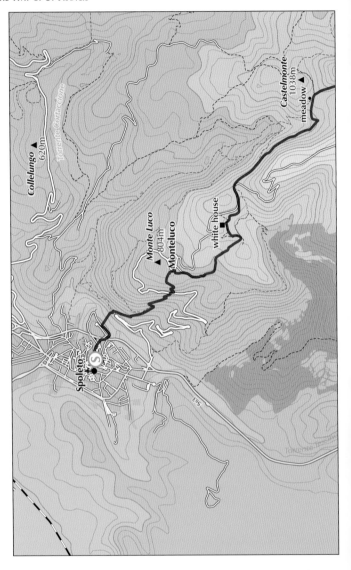

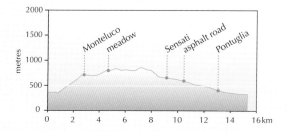

With the beautiful Cathedral of Spoleto at your back, look ahead across the piazza to the grand stairway. Climb the stairway and turn left, crossing under two archways. Soon you see another stairway leading toward the castle; go up the stairway and turn toward the gabled portico on the right. Take the Via del Ponte to the right of the portico and follow it to the viewpoint.

After enjoying the view across green hills to the south of the city, continue past the Hotel Gattapone to the aqueduct that crosses the canyon. Turn right and cross the dramatic 13th-century Ponte delle Torri.

On the other side of the aqueduct turn right, go under the archway and continue uphill along a stone railing. In a couple hundred meters the stone railing and its path veer off to the right. Go left on switchbacks up this very steep climb toward Monteluco, about 40mins ahead, watching carefully for blue-and-yellow Via di Francesco markers.

After a time, come to a gravel road and turn right. Very soon the gravel road turns to asphalt. Continue up, turning left in about 50m at a small shrine. Cross the next gravel road and immediately turn right onto an asphalt road that continues the climb uphill.

In 300m you come to a gravel road at a 'U' switch-back. Go uphill to the left and in 100m come to the driveway of a palazzo. Take the path to the left of the stone wall, then in 250m cross the small highway and find the path with a wooden railing that goes uphill to the left with the sign that says, 'Monteluco: 15 minutes.'

Entry courtyard at the convent of Monteluco (photo: Jacqueline Zeindlinger)

In 500m come to a stone wall on the right. Round the corner and continue uphill where you soon see Hotel Feretti straight ahead (2.7km). At the fork in 100m turn right and come to the parking lot of the hotel and café/bar at **Monteluco**. To the right in 50m are the low roofs of the 13th-century Convento Santuario Monteluco.

St Francis first arrived in **Monteluco** in 1218, seeking solitude with his brothers in the caves. A simple oratorio was built in 1673 over a cave where he lived. Many humble and famous people have found refuge at quiet Monteluco, including St Anthony of Padua, San Bernardino of Siena, St Bonaventure, and Pope Pius IX. In 1556 the 81-year-old artist Michelangelo lived here briefly to rest from his work in Rome.

The Franciscan convent has been remodeled and enlarged many times over the years, but an ongoing Franciscan community is still in residence.

St Francis' oratorio at Monteluco, with the sign 'On this rock St Francis abandoned himself to the Lord.' (photo: Jacqueline Zeindlinger)

Go through the parking lot and turn right toward a café/bar in the park below. ▶ Walk through the field toward the right, looking for a stone tower, then go to the left of the stone tower onto a gravel road. After some homes keep going straight as the road becomes a wide gravel path. At a fork in 100m go left and soon begin uphill again.

Come to an asphalt road at a clearing with a large outdoor fireplace. Go up the asphalt road toward the left and take the path that goes right. Soon you come to a chain link fence and then the driveway of a **white house**. At the house, keep the stone wall on your left and head toward a three-story stone house. Open the gate in the fence and go straight ahead through sometimes-tall grass, looking for a stone marker on the right in 20m. Follow this path to a large open field with an asphalt road on the left and a fenced pasture on the right. ▶ At a 'U' in the asphalt road find a path across a gravel strip to the left; take the path and begin a descent.

This café and the restaurant on the opposite side of the field are your last opportunity before the end of this stage for food and indoor plumbing.

Now you can see sweeping views to the north.

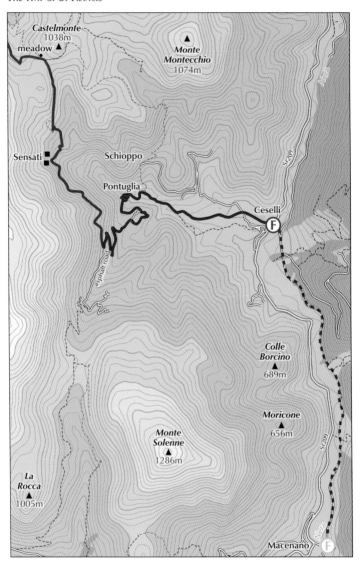

In 400m go straight at the fork that leads to a gradual ascent. The trail becomes a pleasant, earthen track through beech tree woodlands. In 750m come to a **meadow**, which is the summit of today's walk and the best place for a snack or lunch.

After the meadow go straight ahead across the gravel road onto an overgrown path that leads downhill. This is marked as CAI 3, which begins in low brush then passes through trees on a sometimes steep and slippery descent. Breathtaking vistas open up in 300m toward the mountains beyond the steep gorge to the left and the Valnerina (Nera River Valley) to the right.

At a two-track gravel road turn left and in five minutes arrive at the deserted settlement of **Sensati** (9km), with its few remaining stone walls. Continue for quite some time down the sometimes-steep path until you reach an **asphalt road** (11km). Turn left here, following the road for 2.7km first to the village of **Pontuglia** (no services) and then past Casa Vacanze Ruscello to the

Views to the Nera Valley and beyond

The community center in Ceselli

community center of the modern portion of tiny **Ceselli**. (To continue to Macenano and its hotel-restaurant, an additional distance of 5.1km, follow the route description at the beginning of Stage 20.)

CESELLI 317M POP 130

The Nera River stretches from its headwaters in the Sibylline Mountains 116km to Orte, where it flows into the Tiber. Its valley, the Valnerina, includes the Parco Fluvial del Nera, a large protected nature park. The narrow valley is a popular region for hiking, mountain biking, canoeing and kayaking.

Ceselli's older quarter, set above the modern town, includes a Romanesque church dedicated to San Vito and a larger church with an octagonal tower, built in the 16th century and dedicated to St Michael the Archangel. The sleepy village now has an official population of 130 residents.

The resort community of Ceselli has only the agriturismo Casa Vacanze Il Ruscello (Via Contaglia 21, tel 0743 61264, each apartment has a kitchen, €56 cash only, reservation required). The local community association sometimes offers very basic accommodation (tel 0743 613345). If you did not bring your own food, a better option is to continue to the 3 Archi Hotel and Restaurant in Macenano, just 5.1km away on easy paths following the route of Stage 20.

STAGE 20
Ceselli to Arrone

Start	Ceselli community center
Finish	Arrone piazza
Distance	15.5km
Total ascent	221m
Total descent	248m
Difficulty	Easy
Duration	4hrs 45mins

Today features a flat and short walk through the Parco Fluvial del Nera on the Green Way del Nera bike path with the quiet, small towns of Macenano and Precetto/Ferentillo offering food and rest.

Cross the highway out of Ceselli (SS 209) and follow the asphalt road as it makes a gradual turn to the right. In 150m cross the Nera River on a bridge and continue past the last house as the road begins a gentle ascent. In 400m turn right onto a gravel road. In another 500m go left at a fork, following this gravel road, a portion of the Green Way del Nera mountain bike pathway, as it hugs the left side of the valley.

In 1km a road joins from the left and in another 800m go right at the fork toward the green gate. Soon the gravel

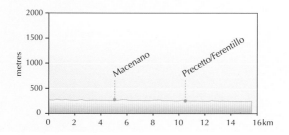

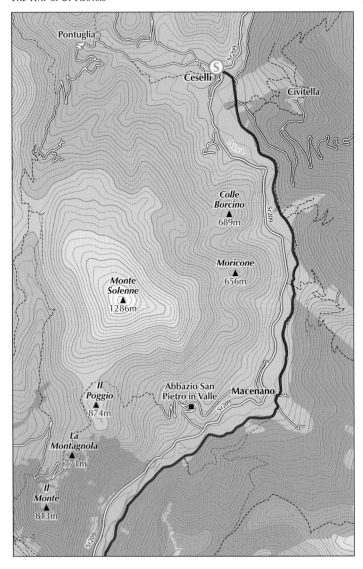

Quiet meadows between mountains in the Valnerina

turns to asphalt and an asphalt road intersects this gravel road. Go straight at the intersection and in 1.8km come to the town of **Macenano** (5.1km) with a seasonal store on this side of the river and the 3 Archi Pizzeria/Restaurant with rooms (Strada Statale Valnerina 29, tel 0744 780004, €25/35) to the right across the bridge and highway. Also available in Macenano, either for a splurge or simply to satisfy curiosity, is the scenic 10th-century **Abbazia San Pietro in Valle** (tel 0744 780129, abbazia@sanpietroinalle. com, €125 double) – a hotel within a restored abbey 800m above town and visible later above the trail.

Leaving the bridge on your right, go straight and follow the large concrete spillway to the left, turning right at the top and then heading straight. The road turns up toward the left, first on broken asphalt and then on gravel. At a triple fork take the right fork that descends slightly down toward the valley and follow this road for 4.6km until it suddenly becomes asphalt and a bridge appears on the right. Go straight, past the restaurant on the left, and enter the town of **Precetto** (10.3km), sister town of

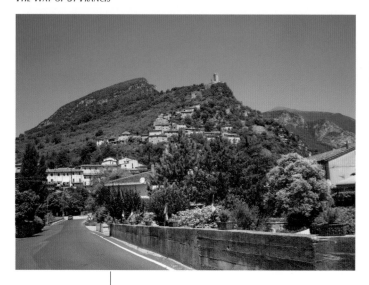

A look across to Ferentillo and its castle from Precetto

Ferentillo across the river, whose castle you have seen for some time on the mountainside. Continue for 300m, veering left to the piazza with its café/bar.

Take the road immediately opposite the piazza and cross a creek. After the bridge turn right at a large tree and rejoin the Green Way del Nera, descending gently between houses. Pass an outdoor sport court structure on the left and continue as the asphalt road turns to gravel.

Follow this road straight through various forks to the left and right until in 3.2km the road turns to asphalt. Turn right at the intersection and go slightly downhill. In 1.2km you come to the parking lot of a mountain bike excursion center at the foot of Arrone. Turn left at the end of the parking area and go under the bridge, then up along the main arterial into the center of town.

At a junction in 100m signs point you toward a Coop supermarket and laundromat on the right. Left is the delightful old city of **Arrone** with its restaurants, farmacia and hotels. Continue left to the main piazza, 100m uphill on the right.

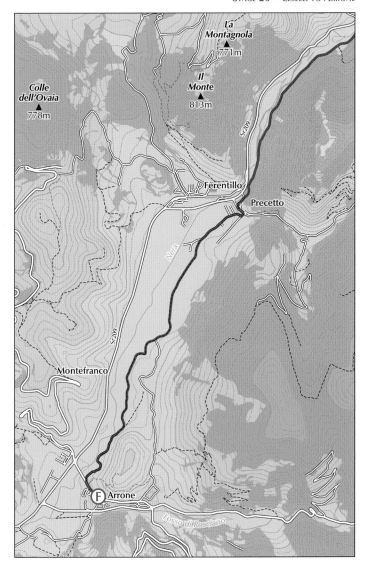

ARRONE 243M POP 2908

A Roman nobleman named Arrone established his namesake town in the ninth century. At first a castle constructed from wood, it was later rebuilt in stone. In the 13th century the army of Spoleto ousted the Arroni and incorporated the town into its Duchy. In 1799 it was sacked and set on fire by the French army under Napoleon. Today the town is a center of the Valnerina recreational area and is known for its celebration of John the Baptist annually on 24 June. Arrone's charming narrow alleys and steep streets lead up to what is left of the medieval castle.

La Loggia Sul Nera (Via Mezzacosta 14, tel 347 4970188, info@loggiasulnera. com, €60 double) is a charming palazzo in the upper city with three terraced apartments. At the foot of town is Case Vacanza Fiocchi (tel 0744 389961, info@ residencefiocchi.com, €45/60 low season), with apartments that include kitchens. The parish of Santa Maria Assunta (Piazza Garibaldi, tel 3339 864664) makes beds available for pilgrims.

STAGE 21
Arrone to Piediluco

Start	Arrone piazza
Finish	Hotel Miralago, Piediluco
Distance	14.5km
Total ascent	294m
Total descent	152m
Difficulty	Moderate
Duration	4hrs 45mins
Note	Carefully schedule your arrival at Cascata delle Marmore to ensure that the impressive waterfall is active when you arrive.

The unforgettable Cascata delle Marmore and serene Lake Piediluco are highlights of today's stage. The walk is flat, both before and after the waterfall, but the path up to the waterfall is extremely steep. The stage follows quiet country roads, pathways and service roads, although a 1.8km stretch is on the narrow shoulder of the SS79 highway.

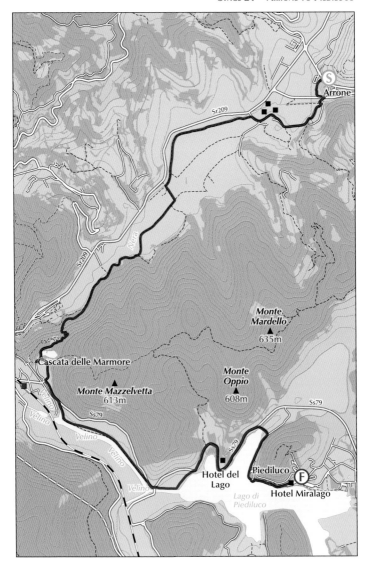

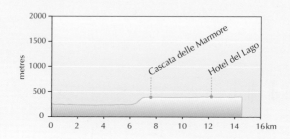

Face the church in the main piazza of Arrone and go straight ahead, passing the church on its left side. Go past a bar and toward a little chapel then turn left, following a long sidewalk downward toward the sports field and, finally, the valley floor.

The path passes Agriturismo La Fiocchi as it curves gradually toward the left, around the base of the mountain on which Arrone is built, until it comes to the main road. Follow the edge of the road down and then turn right and cross it on an underpass. After crossing, turn right again. At the next fork go left and in 50m come to triple fork. Take the middle fork, staying on this asphalt road.

Soon the road cuts through fields, pointing in the direction of the opposite hill town (actually part of Arrone). At the foot of the hill turn right and immediately go right at the next fork on a slow descent through a **grouping of homes**. After crossing a bridge veer left, following the road, and see another valley opening up on the left. Turn right at the fork between two fields and in 100m turn left. Follow this road along the river for 1.9km until it comes to a bridge. Turn left, leaving the bridge on your right, and head toward the forested mountains.

In 300m cross a creek and turn right onto Strada Santa Maria dell Caso, following it for 1km until it ends at a T-junction. Turn right. In 300m the road begins to climb and in another 250m it turns right. However, instead of turning right take the path straight ahead on broken

The Cascata delle Marmora waterfall, looking back toward Arrone and the mountains behind it

asphalt. In 400m go left at the fork, passing through a green gate. In 500m the path becomes quite steep, going uphill quickly on a series of switchbacks. After a second stone bridge go through another green gate and come to a gravel road where you reach the high point of your climb, just 600m after it began.

Turn right onto the gravel road and continue up a gentle hill past a yellow automobile gate. The road now turns to asphalt and on the field to the right you see large surplus turbine parts from the hydroelectric dam at the falls. Continue through the parking lot along the asphalt

Food and services are available at the kiosk plaza or past the ticket office at a restaurant and B&B just before the falls.

drive toward the sports field ahead. Go clockwise around the soccer field and come to the food and souvenir kiosks of the **Cascata delle Marmore**, the hydroelectric dam facility and its mighty waterfalls. ◄

The breathtaking 165m **Cascata delle Marmore** are a creation of the ancient Romans who, in 271BC, chose to divert some of the waters of the Velino River over the natural cliffs at Marmore to drain the swamps around Rieti. Although this solved Rieti's problem, it led to problems at Terni where the Nera River would now sometimes flood its banks, threatening the inhabitants.

In the first century BC the Roman senate debated the problem, with Aulus Pompeius representing Terni and Cicero representing Rieti. But it was not until the 15th–16th centuries that a succession of Popes completed canals and other modifications that resolved the dangerous floods.

In the late 19th century the water flow was harnessed for hydroelectricity, and the falls are switched on and off at certain times of the day when the water flow is directed to power-generating turbines. Scenic viewpoints at intervals on the mountainside ensure a dramatic and refreshing visit (www.marmore.it, €9 – consult the website since the waterfall operates on a variable schedule).

After visiting the kiosks and waterfall head back to the soccer field, turning right just after the field. Follow this drive through a series of parking lots, past a restaurant and, in 300m, come to the highway at the end of the park.

Turn left on the **Strada Statale 79** and look for the walking path on the right side of the guardrail. In 300m turn right into the Campo Sportivo Communale, going through the parking lot toward a shady picnic area. Veer to the right and find the gravel drive along a peaceful canal to the right. Follow this road atop the dike for the next 1.6km, where it ends at the highway. Turn right onto

the highway and cross the intersecting motorway toward a red-and-white gate that leads downhill onto a gravel road once again atop the dike.

Soon you see beautiful Lago Piediluco ahead. The dike road ends and the waymarks lead you toward an overgrown and impassible path. Unless you have a machete, go left toward the cornfield and keep the woods on your right until you come to a well-tended garden. Pick up a new, nicely maintained path to the right of the garden. Follow the path through a wire gate, making certain to close the gate behind you, and then walk toward the driveway that leads up to the shoulder of the main highway.

For the next half-hour you are on the narrow shoulder of the main highway. For a brief respite, walk up the driveway of **Hotel Del Lago** in 800m and follow it to a path on the right, just before the overflow parking lot. Take the path downhill and back onto the highway.

In 600m turn right off the highway onto Piediluco's access road. Cross a small bridge and veer right with the road toward the long, narrow town. In 400m you

Pilgrims walk into Piediluco (photo by Jacqueline Zeindlinger)

can follow a park to the right of the main road, passing a Trattoria, and then you will soon see the tower of the 13th-century Santuario di San Francesco church.

The waymarks point in 100m down to the lake onto a picturesque boardwalk – the Percorso Lungolago – but taking that path means you miss an opportunity to visit the church, built at the site of St Francis' visit to the area. Either way, the path and the main road converge in a few hundred meters. Continue through town to the multi-colored sculpture atop the **Hotel Miralago**, where the day's stage ends.

PIEDILUCO 375M POP 523

The first recorded mention of Piediluco is in 1028, when Castello di Luco was listed as a possession of the Arrone family. A small village sat at the foot of the castle – hence the name, Piediluco. The town's proximity to the Cascata delle Marmore put it on the list of cities to visit in the Grand Tours conducted for European nobility beginning in the 17th century.

The modern town sits on the lakeshore, stretched into a long, thin line against the mountainous rock crowned by the ruined castle. Its historic jewel is the Church of San Francesco, which commemorates the passage of Francis through the territory in 1208. With his brothers, Francis crisscrossed the lake, preaching to the locals. The group built a small mud-and-reed hut on the site of the current church, which houses several interesting frescoes from the 15th–16th centuries.

With the exception of a few modern buildings, the picturesque village remains largely unchanged since the Middle Ages. Its annual Feste delle Acque celebrates boating sports, and the lake is home to the Italian national rowing team, whose sculls can be seen making practice runs during the summer months.

The route passes through the parking lot of the Hotel del Lago Piediluco (Strada del Porto 71, tel 0744 368450, info@hoteldellago.com, from €38), but right in town and situated on the lake is Hotel Miralago (Via Noceta 2, tel 0744 360022, info@miralagohotel.net, seasonal rates from €50/70 includes breakfast). Built in the church's former convent is La Locanda dei Frati (Strada Panoramica 7, tel 0744 369169, riccardobartolucci@tiscali.it, €60/70). Adjacent to the Church of San Francesco is the Casa del Pellegrino with 25 bunk beds for pilgrims and church groups (tel 0744 368118, p.smariadelcolle-piediluco@diocesitna.it).

STAGE 22

Piediluco to Poggio Bustone

Start	Hotel Miralago, Piediluco
Finish	Chiesa San Giovanni Battista, Poggio Bustone
Distance	21.8km
Total ascent	978m
Total descent	662m
Difficulty	Hard
Duration	8hrs
Note	A bar/café in Labro allows an early-morning rest stop, but pilgrims should bring ample food and water and not rely on the restaurant at La Croce (8.1km) that is open on a variable schedule.

The day's first climb is to the tiny, ancient hill town of Labro, one of the unspoiled gems of this pilgrimage. The visit is followed by a steep climb to lofty, tranquil and remote Faggio Bustone – the Beech Tree of St Francis. A long downhill march is rewarded with an overnight in the medieval town of Poggio Bustone with its wide vistas across the Rieti Valley far below and close connection to St Francis.

Starting at Hotel Miralago with its colorful spaghetti giraffe sculptures, head east toward the mountains along

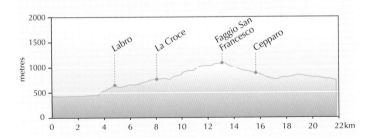

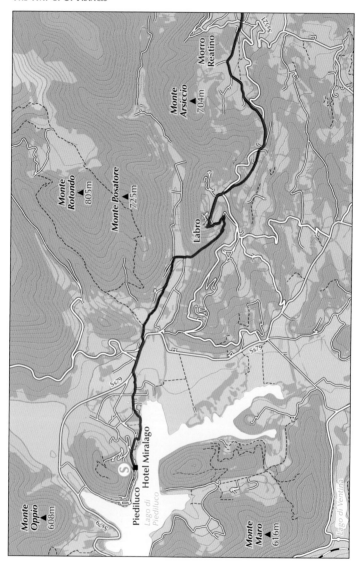

the Corso IV Novembre, the main street of Piediluco. After a parking lot 100m later turn right and take the path along the shoreline through the park. Walk along the shoreline for 200m, turn left on a driveway just before the spectator seating, walk through the parking lot and turn right on the main road.

'Giraffe' sculptures, with the town of Labro atop a mountain in the distance

Pass the Italian National Crew Racing Headquarters and jog slightly right, walking toward the Strada Statale highway. ▶ Pass the next intersection (SP4) and 200m later turn left past a yellow house onto an asphalt road. The road soon turns to gravel and crosses a small bridge. Turn right at the next fork; you've now crossed out of Umbria into the region of Lazio, home to the Eternal City of Rome.

Look toward the mountains to see the hill town of Labro, the first stop on today's itinerary.

Continue straight as the road turns to asphalt in 500m and just after a high-tension electrical power pole turn right, beginning the ascent toward Labro. In 500m go left on the gravel road. At a gate in 100m turn left and begin climbing the hill, which becomes very steep on jagged gravel, dirt and leaves.

After climbing for a time come to a fork in the road: straight ahead the path seems to go in the direction of a gully under trees. Go left instead, taking the grassy road that leads to a wider gravel road. After a steep climb, come to an asphalt road in 300m. Turn left and in another 300m come to the first gate of **Labro** (4.6km). Either enter the gate for a fascinating exploration of the serpentine alleys of this scenic hill town with views below to Lake Piediluco, or continue to the right, following the road directly upward to the café/bar.

Continue 400m beyond the bar to the Carabinieri and come to a fork in the asphalt road. Take the footpath in the middle of the fork going uphill. A steep climb now begins. Turn right at the fork in 300m and soon turn right again onto an asphalt road that you follow for the next 400m. Watch for a waymark that directs you left off the asphalt road onto a gravel road going steeply uphill.

After 200m on the gravel road take the right fork and in 300m come to an asphalt road. Turn right and keep going uphill. In 300m come to an intersection where you turn right onto another asphalt road that leads to a grouping of houses. In another 300m turn right again onto a road that leads slightly uphill. Pass a cemetery on the right and enter the settlement of **La Croce**. Come to the Via Roma and follow it past a pizzeria and butcher shop and past a kiosk with a map of the region.

Just after the butcher shop a road branches to the right. Take the road, which leads by a grey iron gate next to a concrete utility tower. In 500m meet the Via Roma once again, which you follow briefly to the right. Pass the Ristorante di Maria bar and then turn right, followed immediately by a left turn – not onto the highway but onto a road running parallel to the highway just to the right of a Quonset-style building. Go straight ahead at the fork and at the next fork turn right.

You now enter the more remote section of the day's hike. To help your footholds, in 400m the gravel has been covered in asphalt as the road ascends steeply, turning to gravel again in 450m after the steepest portion of the climb. ◄

At this high point enjoy the sweeping views on the right.

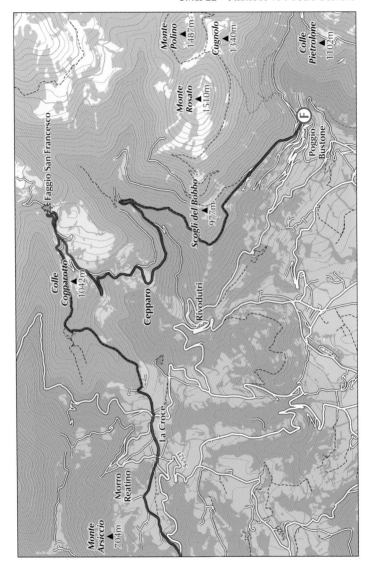

Faggio San Francesco

Continue 700m to a fork. Turn right and continue for 800m where you arrive at a brief downhill stretch. Here look for a path going to the left, marked by two stones with yellow paint. Take this path, watching very carefully for yellow waymarks as you walk just above the asphalt road. Go through a meadow and trees, after which the path traverses the hillside on bedrock. Then watch carefully for yellow marks under the trees that lead you off the nice gravel track. In 100m you see a trail merging with this one – remember it because this is the trail back downhill. Continue uphill to the ridge with the wooden cross on the left.

To the right is an asphalt road, and just left of the road is a path with an X–frame fence leading downhill to the **Faggio San Francesco** beech tree. Follow this path downhill to the ancient tree (12.8km), passing a fork in the path, which you will take uphill after visiting the tree.

Legend says that, while walking through the mountains, Francis was suddenly overwhelmed by a strong storm. Taking shelter under the branches of a **beech tree**, Francis noticed that the tree's branches gathered over him like an umbrella, protecting him from the elements. Francis blessed and thanked the tree, which tradition locates here, at what is confirmed to be one of the oldest living beech trees in the world. Its serpentine shape is unusual for the beech species and its trunk has a maximum circumference of 4m.

After viewing the tree, go back on the trail and take the fork uphill toward the small shrine and chapel. The chapel, although usually locked, has a couple of benches for a much-deserved rest after the challenging climb.

After a rest, take the road left, back toward the wooden cross. At the meadow with the wooden cross turn left and retrace your steps on the path for a very brief time, looking for the fork to the left, which you passed earlier. Take the fork and in 100m come to an asphalt road; cross the road and continue downhill on the path.

Soon you come to two eerie fields of tall thistles. Go along these fields, keeping left of the gully of a seasonal creek. The hard-to-find path follows the fall line of this valley downhill through thick grass. Soon you come to the middle of a switchback of the asphalt road you crossed earlier. Turn left, going downhill, and follow this road all the way to the village of **Cepparo** (15.8km).

At the first switchback after Cepparo, instead of following the road go straight onto a gravel road marked CAI 419. Look for a right turn in 600m where the CAI marker says 'Poggio Bustone: 1 hour.' Turn right onto this path and follow it for 1.8km as it becomes a road.

Soon the CAI markers suggest turning off the road onto a narrow path. Do not take the path, which leads only onto an overgrown and impassable trail: instead stay on the road and follow it as it merges with the Via della Casetta and finally onto the Via San Marco. Continue past the Piazza San Felice and finally to the Porta del Buongiorno, the upper gate of town, by the main parish church and the Municipio of **Poggio Bustone**.

POGGIO BUSTONE 756M POP 2163

Perched high above the Rieti Valley, the well-preserved and picturesque medieval hill town of Poggio Bustone is home to one of the Holy Valley's four main Franciscan sanctuaries. The dramatic setting among steep peaks gives it extraordinary views to the valley below, and the narrow streets and simple stone homes and shops at its center evoke centuries long past.

In 1208, in a small cave above Poggio Bustone now called 'The Grotto of Revelation,' Francis had two important spiritual experiences. In the first he was overwhelmed by a sudden and complete sense of assurance that God had entirely forgiven all his sins. In the second, a dream suffused in light gave him an image of the future. 'I saw a great many men who wanted to share our way of life,' he told his brothers later. 'The roads were filled with Frenchmen, Spaniards, Germans, Englishmen and many others, speaking various languages and hurrying toward us.'

The effect of the experiences was immediately evident in Francis' contagious joy. Coming out of the cave and down the mountain, he entered the town at the gate now aptly called the Porta del Buongiorno and greeted the residents of Poggio Bustone with a cheerful, 'Good day, good people.' The joyful greeting from the simple man is well remembered to this day and commemorated on a stone slab in the heart of the village.

The 12th-century Convent of San Giacomo atop the town includes several small medieval chapels and cells. To reach the convent, go directly uphill from the Porta del Buongiorna. A stairway above the convent leads to the Grotto of Revelation.

Feliciano joyfully welcomes pilgrims at La Locanda Francescana (Via Francescana 13, tel 0746 688688, info@locandafrancescana.com, from €25). Ask for directions to the rooms, which are a few blocks below on Poggio's winding streets. With advance notice, beds are available at the Santuario Francescano (tel 0746 688916, convpbustone@libero.it), which is located about 700m above town in the Convento San Giacomo.

STAGE 23

Poggio Bustone to Rieti

Start	Chiesa di San Giovanni Battista, Poggio Bustone
Finish	Piazza Vittorio Emanuel II, Rieti
Distance	17.7km
Total ascent	395m
Total descent	745m
Difficulty	Moderate
Duration	6hrs

The day includes a lovely walk through forests, fields and farms to the charming hill town of Cantalice, followed by a visit to the beloved Santuario La Foresta. While the last two kilometers into Rieti are urban, the central city offers shopping, restaurants, a rich history and a beautiful cathedral.

In the piazza between Poggio Bustone's parish church and its Municipio, with the archway to your back, turn right, finding the marked path that goes downhill first on steps and then on grey paving stones. In 40m go right on a concrete drive, which then turns left going downhill.

Aim at the bottom of the hill to the left and come to a flat spot in the road. Turn right on the road and pass a

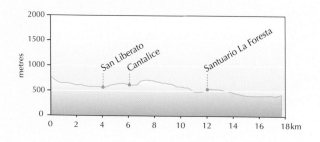

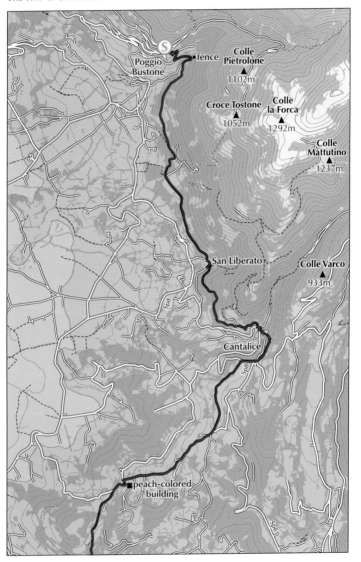

Tau symbol on the sidewalk. Continuing downhill, take a fork to the left. Soon the sidewalk goes from pavement to concrete to asphalt and then becomes a gravel path. Take the gravel path with the wooden **X–frame fence** and follow the fence line down and ultimately across the valley below town.

Cross a small bridge where now you can see the first of many views back to Poggio Bustone. The path soon becomes a two-track gravel road. Turn left at the fork, following the X–frame fence with the sign 'Santuario La Foresta' and 'Tomba di Pietro 117km.' Turn left in 1.4km at a gravel road that joins the path and then begin a moderately steep climb.

In 100m the road turns left and becomes a driveway. Turn right onto a gravel path going downhill. At the fork in 300m go straight, coming to the edge of the forest. Soon the gravel road ends at an asphalt road facing a large pasture. Turn right here and then immediately turn left, following this road for 1.5km until it makes a hairpin turn at a group of houses in the tiny town of **San Liberato** (4km).

Turn left here, watching carefully for signs that point to a driveway going uphill between two buildings. In 375m go right at a fork onto a narrow earthen path under trees, which undulates upward 1.3km toward a ridge. Go straight after a fountain and soon a house appears on the right side. Continue onto the road in front of the house and see the picturesque hill town of Cantalice across the valley ahead.

Turn right onto the concrete road and follow it downhill to the asphalt road. In a few meters turn left onto another asphalt road, winding downhill to the main auto road into Cantalice. Turn left into the main piazza of lower **Cantalice** with its café/bar (6km).

Take the stairway to the right of the café/bar and wind your way upward through Cantalice to the piazza and fountain in front of the large, yellow, 19th-century Church of San Felix. Turn right at the fountain and follow the walkway that soon becomes a road going along the ridge out of town, passing homes and a bakery. Go right

*Cantalice, seen
from below*

*Rieti is visible in
the distance in the
valley below.*

at the end of the road toward a bar. Pass the bar and go
left at the next fork. ◄

The road now follows the ridgeline downhill. Soon
you come to an intersection: go straight and 50m later
at a fork with two asphalt roads turn right. In 500m at
another fork stay left, going uphill. The road starts going
downhill in 200m and in another 500m a road goes off to
the left with a tempting yellow marker. Go straight. After
a gravel road a steep descent begins. Pass a sign that says
'La Foresta: 2.5km.'

The road suddenly turns right just before a **peach-
colored building** (9.5km). Instead, take the road to the
left that is just in front of the building, going downhill on
asphalt. Now the road winds its way downward between
farm buildings. After the farm turn left on the gravel road.

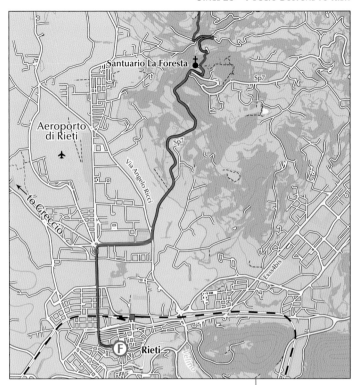

In 300m, after the last two houses, the road narrows to a mildly overgrown path. Go left at the fork in 400m, walking steeply downhill on gravel. The path ends at a gravel road in front of a house with an odd tower on top. Turn left. Soon an asphalt road joins the gravel road; take this road in a leftward direction. At a fork in a couple hundred meters go right and uphill, then take another right turn following the guardrail around to cross a creek.

After a time, X–framed fences appear again on the right. Turn right onto a path that goes uphill and in 300m go left toward the side of a building. You have arrived at **Santuario La Foresta** (12km).

*Inner courtyard of
Santuario La Foresta*

Late in his life, an illness in his eyes caused Francis to gradually lose his sight. Cardinal Ugolino of Rieti begged him to come to his town to undergo treatment from a prominent doctor nearby; but large crowds had begun to follow Francis. Needing rest and a respite from the crowds, he chose to remain at the nearby church of **San Fabiano**.

He stayed here for more than 50 days as the crowds assembled in the surrounding vineyards, consuming nearly the entire year's crop of grapes. The local farmers, seeing that their livelihood was destroyed, entreated Francis to do something. According to legend he had them bring their remaining grapes to the winepress at the church and to their astonishment, after pressing the grapes the winepress yielded double the juice it had in the previous year's crop. This became known as 'the Miracle of the Wine,' and San Fabiano's ultimately became a Franciscan convent called La Foresta – the guesthouse. People who suffer from

drug and alcohol abuse now receive treatment at
the convent's Communitá Mondo X.

Leave the church behind you and go straight ahead
on the asphalt driveway that sweeps in a circle to the
right, around fields and vineyards with Stations of the
Cross on tiles at intervals. At the gate go straight onto Via
Foresta, a two-lane asphalt road leading downhill. Follow
this road until you come to an intersection with the main
arterial, **Via Angelo Ricci** (15.2km).

Cross the road after the traffic circle and take an
immediate right onto Viale Giulio de Juliis, a wide boulevard with apartment blocks on both sides. Cross to the
left and at the next traffic circle turn left onto Via Marco
Curio Dentato. Follow this road 1.2km straight toward
the city walls. Cross the Viale Ludovico Canali into the
old city and go straight ahead onto the Via Cintia, which
curves toward the left and leads in 500m to the piazza of
the Duomo of **Rieti**. After visiting this beautiful cathedral,
continue another block to Piazza Vittorio Emanuel, the
end of the stage.

RIETI 405M POP 47,927

The ancient the town of Rieti traces its roots to the ninth through eighth centuries
BC. Romans subsumed the town and its surrounding Sabine region and, according
to legend, abducted its women to serve the purposes of Roman men. The 'Rape of
the Sabines' is a common theme in Renaissance art.

In the 12th century AD Saracens sacked Rieti, and in the 20th century the
town was partially destroyed in Allied bombardment. Much of the 13th-century
medieval wall still stands, particularly on the north side of the city, and continues
to shelter its quaint streets.

The Duomo of Rieti and its tower, built between the 13th and 16th centuries
and dedicated to Santa Maria Assunta, mark the center of town, and the narrow
pedestrian streets on the downward slope to the Velino River hold prosperous
shops. An unusual archaeological feature is Underground Rieti, where portions
of the ancient Roman salt road, the Via Salaria, can be seen. On the riverfront
stands the historic Chiesa di San Francesco (13th century) with its frescoes from
the school of Giotto depicting the life of St Francis.

Interior of the Duomo of Rieti

Near Rieti are two important Franciscan sanctuaries: at Fonte Colombo Francis completed his rule for communal life in 1222–1223, remaining there six weeks while he dictated its contents to his followers. Here also in 1224 doctors cauterized Francis' eyes in an attempt to cure his illness. Although his disciples could not bear to watch the branding of his eyes, Francis insisted he could not feel any pain at all. The serene Santuario Fonte Colombo sits above Rieti among the lush oak forests of Mount Rainiero, and can be reached from Piazza Cavour on Line 333 of the ASM Rieti bus service in just 15 minutes (www.asmrieti.it). About 15km from Rieti, the steep cliffs at Greccio offered cataracts favored by Francis for solitude and meditation. Here, on Christmas Eve of 1223, Francis brought together farm animals, a manger and villagers to recreate the scene of Christ's birth at Bethlehem. The tradition of Christmas manger or crèche scenes spread from Greccio throughout the world. The sanctuary is a 40min bus ride via San Marco from Rieti's Viale Marroni on the Cotral bus service (www.cotralspa.it).

In Piazza Vittorio Emanuel is the aging but elegant Grande Albergo Quattro Stagioni (Piazza Cesare Battisti 14, tel 0746 271071, info@hotelquattrostagionirieti.it, from €60). Less expensive and also nearby is Hotel Europa (Via San Rufo 49, tel 0746 495149, hoteleuroparieti@virgilio.it, €40/50). Near the train station is Casa Simonetti B&B (Viale Maraini 5, tel 0746 483396, info@casasimonetti.net, €20). Overnight accommodation for pilgrims is available at Santuario La Foresta (tel 0746 200727), although it is 5.5km from the center of Rieti.

4 RIETI
TO ROME

Inside the nature preserve of Marcigliana (Stage 27)
(photo: Jacqueline Zeindlinger)

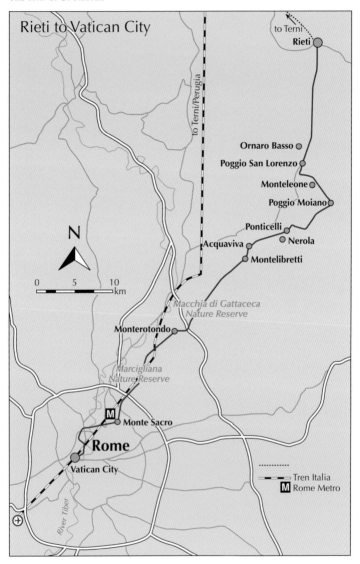

Rieti to Vatican City

to Terni

Rieti

to Terni/Perugia

Ornaro Basso

Poggio San Lorenzo

Monteleone

Poggio Moiano

Ponticelli

Acquaviva   Nerola

Montelibretti

N

0   5   10
km

*Macchia di Gattaceca
Nature Reserve*

Monterotondo

*Marcigliana
Nature Reserve*

Ⓜ

Monte Sacro

Rome

Vatican City

River Tiber

⊕

.... Tren Italia
Ⓜ Rome Metro

Looking back toward Rieti from the hill near Ornaro Basso (Walk 24)

Although the last 120km of the Way of St Francis from Rieti to Rome include fewer scenes from the life of St Francis, they are full of wonder nevertheless. The route carries pilgrims through vast, protected forestland, into nature preserves filled with wildlife, along archeological digs of ancient cities, and under the sleepy but watchful eye of medieval castles.

The pilgrim route crosses from the Rieti plain over a low ridge of the Central Apennines, through the region of Sabina, known worldwide for the premium quality of its olive oil. The area is dotted with small, proud towns, each with its own history traced back to the Romans and beyond. The memories of Roman generals, noble aristocrats, reclusive saints, marauding hordes, and heroes of the Italian resistance still echo among the narrow streets of towns like Monteleone and Montelibretti.

After Ponticelli the mountains gradually give way to the vast and fertile Tiber River plain. Here the itinerary passes through the protected wilderness areas of Riserva Macchia di Gattaceca and Riserva Naturale della Marcigliana, home to deer, squirrels, foxes and boars, not to mention many species of deciduous trees and plant life.

After a penultimate half-day of walking on sidewalks next to busy streets, the final day's route follows a bicycle path along first the Aniene and then the famed Tiber River. The climax of the walk comes with an entry along the colonnaded Piazza San Pietro to one of the most spectacular and beloved buildings in the world – Saint Peter's Basilica. The experience of Christian Rome will become deeper as pilgrims spend a day walking to the Seven Pilgrim Churches of Rome.

STAGE 24
Rieti to Poggio San Lorenzo

Start	Piazza Vittorio Emanuel II, Rieti
Finish	Agriturismo Santa Giusta, Poggio San Lorenzo
Distance	21.8km
Total ascent	499m
Total descent	377m
Difficulty	Moderate
Duration	7hrs
Note	The only option for lunch is Ornaro Basso, a detour of 1km off the trail.

A mostly flat and mellow stage that walks along creeks and fields into forests, ending with some steep climbs just before tiny Poggio San Lorenzo.

Straight ahead within a block are a grocery store, fruit store, cash machine and café/bar.

From Rieti's main square, Piazza Vittorio Emanuele II, walk downhill along the shops of Via Roma toward the river. Cross the Velino River and come to a piazza. ◀ Just before the piazza turn left, keeping the park on your right, and walk across the transit center toward the large church. Cross the Strada Salaria on the right of the church and then turn right at the war memorial onto Via Borgo Sant'Antonio. Follow this road across Via Giacomo Matteotti as it becomes Via Fonte Cottorella.

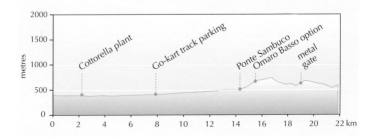

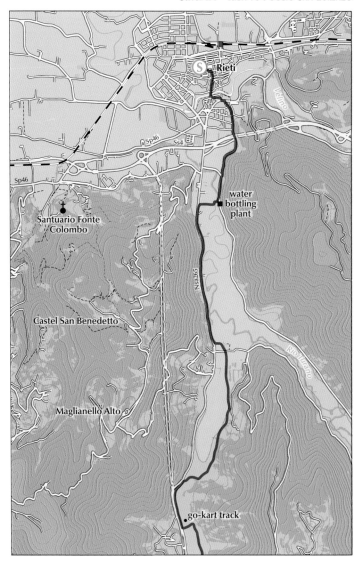

Pass under the highway bridge and continue to the **Cottorella water bottling plant** (2.2km) on the left. Just across the road is the '100 Kilometers to Rome' waymark sign. Continue 200m until a trail appears on the right and follow the trail, going down the bank through undergrowth. Cross a wooden bridge and turn left, following a green chain link fence. Round the corner of the fence to the right and follow the path until it comes to a row of trees at the SS4bis highway ahead.

Turn left at the highway and soon come to a gas station with a bar. Continue 1.8km on the pleasant and safe path along the shoulder of the tree-lined highway until the waymark points you to the left. Turn left and after 25m turn right on a gravel road that follows the fence around a hayfield and then to an asphalt road. Go straight ahead onto the path with wooden railings along the creek and follow the path for 1.9km until it ends at a two-track gravel road.

Turn right and follow the road back to the highway. Turn left on the path just before the road and follow this path along the highway for 700m, past a **go-kart track and parking lot**. Just after the parking lot follow the waymark pointing left onto an asphalt road.

Continue on the asphalt road past a stone house, then cross the bridge and turn right on the gravel track with the same wooden railing as before. The path now becomes overgrown with brambles, but after just 700m it widens to become a gravel road. Take the road past a pasture and hayfield on the left until it ends at an asphalt road. Turn left and 200m later come to a fork in the road. Take the gravel road to the right.

In 600m the road changes to asphalt at the beginning of an undeveloped subdivision. Turn left in 500m onto a quiet asphalt road between hayfields, sunflower fields and barns. Follow this road for 2.6km to a fork and take the gravel fork downhill to the right. In 300m stay right at the fork. At the bottom of the hill cross the creek on stones. Just afterward turn left and walk through the field toward picnic benches and a kiosk at the fourth-century **Ponte Sambuco** Roman bridge (14.4km).

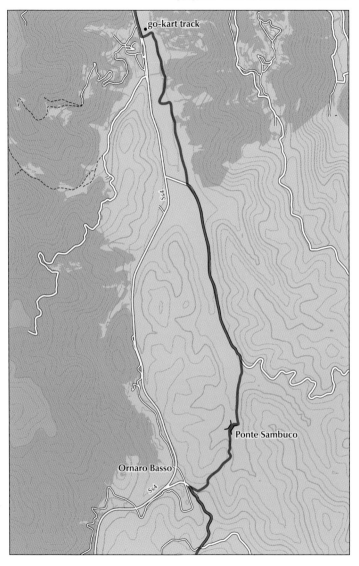

225

The charming Piazza Vittorio Emanuele II and Quattro Stagione Hotel of Rieti

To the right of the picnic area is a path that leads up a bank. Scramble up the bank and turn left, crossing the Roman bridge. Follow the road steeply uphill as it climbs to a summit in 1.2km where you can look back over the fields and pastures behind.

Soon you come to a small settlement with a few scattered houses. The road turns right and goes downhill to the highway; here you have the option of taking the road to the right leading in 500m to the town of **Ornaro Basso** with its restaurant, bar and tobacco shop. Otherwise continue left on the highway and follow it gently uphill for 1km. At the pizzeria veer right off the highway and take the small asphalt road going downhill (16.7km). Follow this road on switchbacks over gravel, concrete and asphalt for 1.3km to the bottom of the valley.

At the bottom of the hill is a creek and then a fork. Go left under trees and in 500m come to an intersection with a gravel road. Go straight. At the bottom of the hill take the grassy road to the left of the gate, walking downhill to a seasonal creek. Cross the creek and continue on the path as it climbs on a pleasant woodland trail with a creek on the right.

Agriturismo Santa Giusta near Poggio San Lorenzo

In a few hundred meters cross the creek on the rickety bridge, or perhaps cross more safely on stones. Above a somewhat forsaken clear-cut in 200m come to a **metal gate** at a wide gravel road (18.9km). Turn left and follow the road for 200m to an asphalt road at the bottom of a hairpin turn. Although the waymarks point left, turn right instead and continue 1.7km to the turnoff for **Agriturismo Santa Giusta**, which can be found about 700m off the road. Otherwise go straight ahead and arrive in 700m at Poggio San Lorenzo.

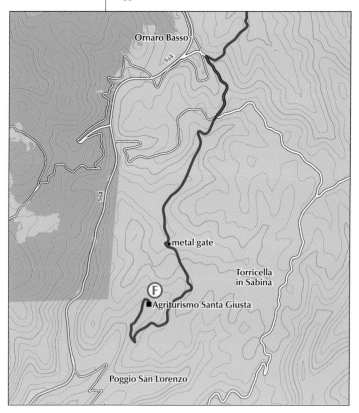

POGGIO SAN LORENZO 492M POP 565

The ancient Roman walls of tiny Poggio San Lorenzo buttress the town's flank and are still visible below the piazza, showing intricate Roman brickwork over 2000 years old.

Most often used by pilgrims is the quiet and remote Agriturismo Santa Giusta (tel 339 4984008, astroste@hotmail.it, from €35/70), which also has dining room with a fixed-price menu. Le Casette Pizzeria (Via Quinzia 202, tel 0765 880353) offers another option for the evening meal. At 4km after Poggio San Lorenzo is B&B Locanda Sabina (tel 0756 884434, from €20).

STAGE 25
Poggio San Lorenzo to Ponticelli

Start	Agriturismo Santa Giusta, Poggio San Lorenzo
Finish	Piazza del Sole, Ponticelli
Distance	23.2km
Total ascent	821m
Total descent	1015m
Difficulty	Hard
Duration	8hrs 30mins
Notes	The lack of accommodation options in Ponticelli means that pilgrims need to make arrangements elsewhere (see information given under 'Ponticelli' at the end of the route description).

Although a long stage with some steep hills, the day also offers some spectacular mountain scenery and very pleasant walks through orchards, fields and farms. Historic sites and small villages like Monteleone and Poggio Moiano are noteworthy diversions along the way.

Leave the Santa Giusta Agriturismo and return uphill to the main road, the Via Quinzia. Turn right and in 100m is Le Casette restaurant/pizzeria and in another 400m are

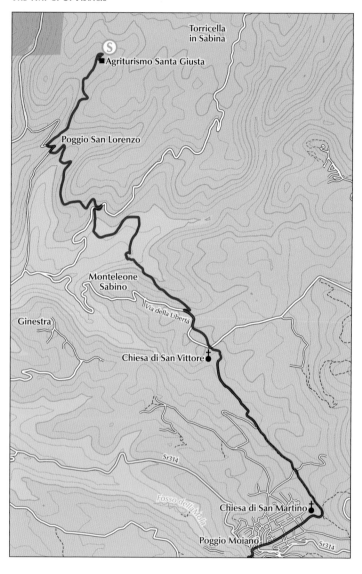

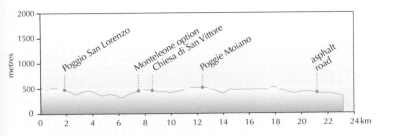

outskirts of **Poggio San Lorenzo**. Soon the road turns to cobblestone, leading to the pleasant piazza with its café and shops before leading out of town. Past the piazza at a children's play area turn left, going downhill.

At the following hairpin turn you have the option of walking left just 50m and inspecting ancient brickwork of the Roman Walls of San Lorenzo. Afterwards continue down the road on switchbacks leading to the bottom of the valley. Turn right in 200m after the last switchback onto a road with broken concrete paving. Follow this road to the bottom of the hill and then veer left and uphill. You can now look back on Poggio San Lorenzo high above. Stay on this road to the summit, where it becomes overgrown as it skirts olive groves to the right. Pass a brown stucco house and then walk straight ahead to another house with a chain link fence. The road now turns left and winds downhill where it comes to a gate. After wriggling past the gate come to an asphalt road and turn right.

In a few meters the signage points you to a pathway across the road. Because this path becomes impassable, instead follow the road rightward around a curve and then a second curve until a dirt road appears on the left. Follow this road as it winds to the right and downhill. Come to a fork in the road and continue downhill. In 100m you come to a large field on the right with an overgrown road going straight toward the bottom of the valley. At the fork in 700m at the bottom of the valley, go left

The day's walk includes a series of ridges, this one looking out toward Monteleone

to cross a bridge. In 100m go left on a second fork and cross a creek on stones.

In 500m a path joins from the right. Continue straight and come to a green gated shed. Continue uphill to the right of the shed. In 300m the path turns to concrete and becomes steeper. It goes back to gravel and once again to concrete before it intersects with a small asphalt road in 700m. Turn right and in 100m the markers tell you to turn left onto the **Via della Libertá** road (7.7km). However, with a right turn you can go to **Monteleone Sabina**, whose quiet streets offer shade and refreshments. ◀

If you take this pleasant diversion, once in town turn right at the fork to find the main piazza and afterwards retrace your steps to the turnoff.

From the turnoff, continue on the Via della Libertá toward the cemetery and then turn right at the fork and go downhill. In 150m turn left toward the first- to ninth-century archeological project Trebula Mutuesca. Just after the former visitors' center take the path along the edge of the fence then turn right along the corner of the fence into a meadow.

Hug the left side of the meadow, aiming for two trees and a stone house on the other side. Go to the right of the stone house and then veer right. Stay on this road for 30m then turn right at a white crucifix onto the asphalt road that goes downhill. Look for the fourth- to 12th-century **Chiesa di San Vittore** on the right.

The historic **San Vittore church** shelters the sar-cophagus of the fourth-century martyr Vittore inside in a small catacomb. Also inside the church is a small well whose waters are said to have healing properties. Intricate stone sculptures in the façade help make the church an architectural gem.

After visiting San Vittore continue downhill steeply on the curving road, past the memorial for locals killed by Nazis in World War II, to the bottom of the hill. At the next fork go uphill to the left on asphalt, continuing on the road as it begins downhill, crosses a creek, and continues uphill with orchards on the left. The road continues to climb and, at a switchback, comes to a fork. Go left, following vineyards uphill and then into a wood. At a fence on the right in 600m go uphill on jagged rocks.

Turn left at an asphalt road in 200m and follow the road to the right along an olive grove. Continue on this road for 700m to an asphalt road with no direction signs. Turn right here. Continue around the bowl-shaped valley past the ancient stone **Chiesa di San Martino** (built in the 10th century) and uphill up toward Poggio Moiano.

San Vittore Church near Monteleone

233

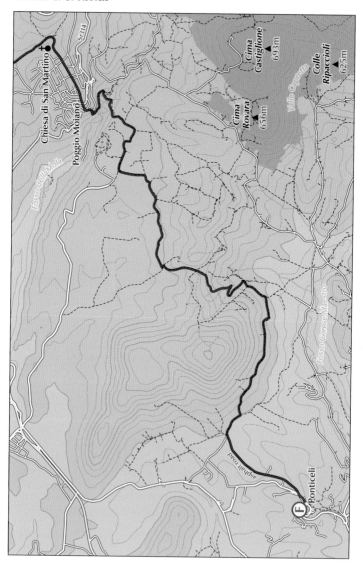

Cross the Via Circovallazione Moianense onto Via Piazza Giovanni XXIII, a wide suburban drive through two-story homes with iron fences. Stay straight as the road leads across the Via Lichinese into the central piazza of **Poggio Moiano** (13km) with its bars, banks and other services.

Turn left at the main piazza and pass to the left of the church, going downhill on pink paving stones. The pink pavers end at a mural of three maidens where you turn right onto a white concrete-and-stone drive. Soon there is a switchback to the left and once more pink pavers guide the path.

Turn left at Via Scandriglia. The road soon turns to a ragged path of jagged stones. Go past the fountain to the creek below; at the bottom of the valley the road turns right across an ancient stone bridge. After the bridge continue on the road as it veers to the left past a house.

The road now turns to concrete and goes extremely steeply uphill. At the top of the walk, opposite the town, the path becomes a pleasant two-lane gravel road under trees. In 300m after the summit turn right on a gravel road; in 120m turn right at a sheepfold; and then in 150m turn right again. In 100m turn left at the intersection and in 400m turn left again. In 400m come to another intersection and turn right. Follow this road for 900m until an intersection. Turn left (uphill) at this intersection.

Poggio Moiano, seen from the trail

235

Going downhill toward Ponticelli, with sheep on the neighboring pasture

Wide vistas now open up among olive orchards, with mountains ahead. The road now goes downhill on a series of switchbacks and in 1.8km comes to an intersection with barns on the left. Take the right-most turn onto the smaller, unmarked road, which is easily missed. A steep climb begins in 75m. Continue straight, with sweeping views of Scandriglia and surrounding mountains to the left, and turn right at the next fork, going slightly uphill. In 200m come to a fence on the left side, and then a gravel road that you follow for 1.8km until it ends at an **asphalt road** (21.3km).

Turn right on the asphalt road, noting Castel Orsini on the opposite hillside. At a fork in the road with a white house in the middle go left. Pass the cemetery on the right and walk downhill 1.5km to the main piazza of **Ponticelli** and its church and bar/pizzeria.

PONTICELLI 300M POP 515

Ponticelli may be more memorable for what is near it than for the tiny village itself. Across the valley is majestic Castello Orsini of the late Middle Ages, as well as tiny but scenic village of Scandriglia. Just below Ponticelli is the 15th-century Santa Maria della Grazie, a Franciscan sanctuary that houses 'The Pearl of Sabina' – a recently restored icon of the Virgin Mary (www.santuariodisan tamariadellegrazie.org).

Since Ponticelli has no hotel or B&B, one option is to arrange for a hotel in a nearby town to pick you up in the afternoon and return you to Ponticelli the next morning. Salaria Hotel (Via Salaria, Osteria Nuova, tel 0765 841056, info@salariahotel.it, €55) is 15 minutes away and will pick you up. Or, an additional walk of 4.3km brings you to Villa Viola B&B (tel 0774 683304, €36/52). Off the track 3km south of Ponticelli is Agriturismo La Ripa, near the convent of Santa Maria dell Grazie (Locanda Santa Maria, Montorio Romano, 077 462174, from €60). Another option is to speak to the La Torre pizzeria proprietor (tel 0765 896009) across from the church in Ponticelli and ask about the possibility of staying at the church itself, which offers free beds to pilgrims. An unusual treat is an overnight at Castel Orsini (Via Aldo Bigelli 54, Nerola, tel 077 4683272, direzione@castelloorsini.it, from €47), which has a commanding view from its high stone walls and can be seen for many miles. It is a 16km trip to Ponticelli for the hotel staff, but by walking the 4.8km to Nerola (see Stage 26) the staff's trip is reduced to just a couple of kilometers.

STAGE 26
Ponticelli to Monterotondo

Start	Piazza del Sole, Ponticelli
Finish	Fausto Cecconi memorial, Monterotondo
Distance	29.8km
Total ascent	690m
Total descent	871m
Difficulty	Moderate
Duration	8hrs

Leading down from the mountains into the widening Tiber Valley plain, this long and undulating stage on gravel and asphalt roads stretches through orchards and farmland, crossing the towns of Acquaviva and Montelibretti and the nature reserve of Macchia di Gattaceca. The reward is central Monterotondo and its delightful pedestrian mall and old city.

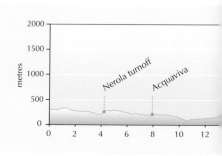

In the main piazza of Ponticelli, with the bar to right, go straight ahead. Soon you walk downhill, past a tall stone wall. At the first fork go steeply downhill to the right. At the fork at the bottom of the hill go left and continue straight ahead when a main road appears from the

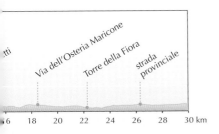

left. Go straight onto Via San Martino uphill on the right above the main road.

At a right fork between two houses go right. Go up a little rise then steeply downhill. The asphalt road quickly turns to concrete, which then curves right. Take the next

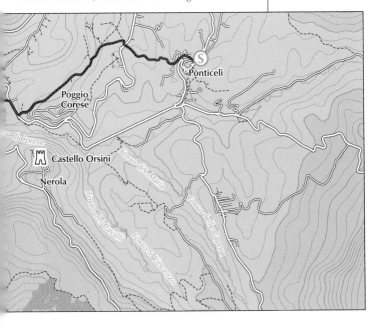

First views of Montelibretti on the hilltop

fork left, going downhill, and continue to the Via Salaria Vecchia (1.2km).

Cross this asphalt road, going downhill at first on concrete. At the fork in 75m go left and at another fork in 500m go left again. Continue until the gravel road ends at the bottom of a switchback of an asphalt road in the town of **Poggio Corese**. Go downhill to the right on this road, the Strada Provinciale per Orvinio, which soon ends at a T-junction with the Via Salaria Vecchia (3.2km). Turn right and go 200m, past a Trattoria on the right, and then turn left onto an earthen path leading slightly downhill.

Watch carefully for an unmarked left turn in 200m onto an asphalt road. Go downhill and in 50m cross a bridge and ascend a very steep hill. The Villa Viola B&B is in 400m and shortly afterward the Strada Provinciale 28A. (To the left is the town of Nerola and the quickest access to the Castel Orsini hotel, which has been visible on the hill for some time.)

Cross the highway and continue in the direction of Localita Ferrari. In 300m a road joins from the right and just afterward a left fork leads to an agriturismo. Go right.

In 750m the road ends at an intersection with an asphalt road. Turn right, going slightly downhill through olive orchards, and enjoy the beautiful vistas ahead toward Montelibretti.

At a fountain in 600m turn right and continue 400m until the road ends at an asphalt road. Turn left and at a fork in 500m go left again. Pass a plant nursery on the left and in 400m come to a main arterial. Turn right (direction Salaria) and enter the town of **Acquaviva** with its restaurants, bars and fruit shop. At the familiar and now busy Via Salaria Vecchia turn left and then take the left fork at the first intersection.

Continue on this road for 800m past a fountain under two pine trees and take the left fork. In 400m make a right turn at a green gate. The road descends steeply to an asphalt road in 700m. Cross the road and go straight, with views of the old portion of Montelibretti at the top of the hill. Soon you come to the bottom of the descent and cross a creek on a culvert.

Just after you begin climbing from the valley floor stay left at the fork. Continue ahead and cross the Strada Provinciale 20b then continue 500m to the Via delle Terre Sabine. Turn right and climb very steeply past an olive oil factory. Veer right and then turn left at the top of the hill at Strada Provinciale 26a toward the very welcome café/bar and bakery on the outskirts of **Montelibretti** (13.2km).

Turn onto Via Vignacce, between the bar and bakery, and soon come to a quadruple fork. Take the middle fork, Via Valle Spaziani, going straight ahead. Just after a little rise is a fork, which you follow left along a concrete wall. The road then winds around an olive grove. Go left at the second fork and stay on this asphalt road as it leads down and out of Montelibretti. ▶

Soon the road goes steeply downhill and in 400m comes to an unmarked fork. Go right, continuing downhill. At an intersection in 200m, turn left. Stay straight, and in 700m turn right at the fork. In a further 100m take the left fork.

You come to the floor of the valley in 200m, entering woods as you begin climbing up for the next 100m.

The towns of Palombara Sabina and Guidonia are visible on hills in the distance to the left.

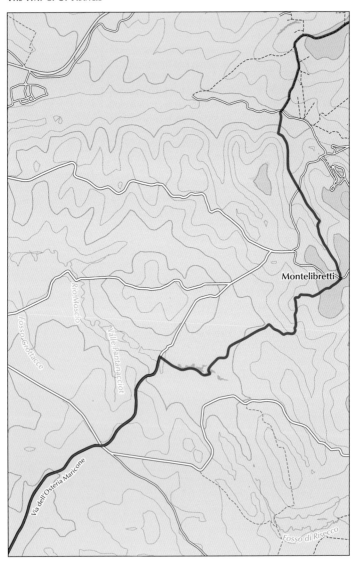

Just after the woods turn right at a chain link fence onto a grassy drive. Continue along the fence, past the gate and down the driveway along the fence. Turn left onto asphalt Via Vecchia Nomentana at an unmarked intersection in 100m.

Stay on this historic Roman road, which ascends steeply, and avoid other roads from the right and left until the summit in 900m. You come to a main road in another 700m with a business park on the left. Turn right here (unmarked) onto the asphalt **Via dell'Osteria di Maricone** (18.6km). Continue along this road until it intersects the Strada Provinciale 35d. Cross the highway and go to the left of a white house with brown shutters on the Via Santa Maria delle Camere. ▶

The Macchia di Gattaceca Nature Reserve is just ahead.

In 900m the road begins to descend steeply to the bottom of the valley and then turns left past a derelict, ancient stone house. It then veers right and comes to a creek. Cross the creek on a bridge and then turn right onto a long, straight road that goes gradually uphill, noting the brick **Torre della Fiora** watch tower, which dates from the 13th century, on the right. The flat road soon turns left and begins a 100m climb. At the top of the climb take the right fork, going downhill. In 500m the

Torre della Fiora in the Macchia di Gattaceca nature reserve

road turns right and heads uphill after passing gates on the left and right sides.

In 1km you come to a summit. The road continues straight ahead and in 300m, when a road from the left joins, it becomes an asphalt road. Go straight ahead, past a barn on the right and past a road that intersects from the left.

In 1.4km this peaceful road under Roman pines comes to a busy arterial. Turn right and then 50m later turn right again briefly onto the **SP25a highway** (26.2km). Across the valley you can now see Monterotondo, as well as the A1 Autostrada del Sole standing in the way.

Rather than crossing the Autostrada on the highway, in 200m get off the busy SP25a at a fork to the right that leads to a restaurant parking lot. Here follow the yellow arrows leading circuitously but safely down to the highway. Cross under the Autostrada on the sidewalk and follow the yellow arrows after the bridge, which lead to a path that follows the fence along the Autostrada.

Turn left on an asphalt path that leads back toward the two-lane highway and in 100m go straight, again following the yellow markers. Cross the metal bridge and come to an overgrown and thorny path between a metal pasture fence and the metal mesh fence of the highway. Continue 600m on this difficult path (unless the trail gods have commanded it be mowed) until you come back to the highway. Follow the metal grate sidewalk along the highway to the stoplight at the Strada Provinciale 25b (27.8km).

Here you have a choice of two options for reaching the historic center of Monterotondo.

Official route
The longer official route goes to the left on the green bike path, turning right at the Via Nomentana to reach the center.

Shortcut
Go straight up the hill on Via Castelchiodato and then Via Giuseppe Mazzini into the center.

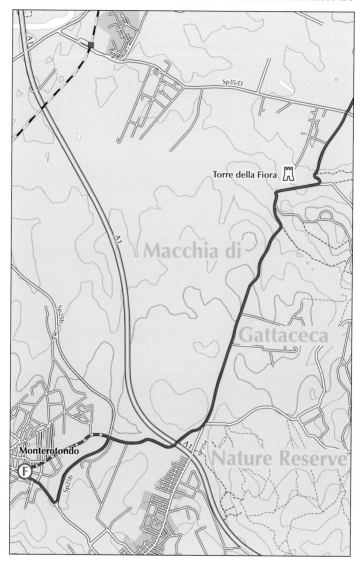

Both paths lead to opposite ends of **Monterotondo**'s delightful Passegiata pedestrian mall. The stage ends at the Memorial to Fausto Cecconi, at the southeast end of the mall.

MONTEROTONDO 165M POP 40,771

Although the site of the ancient city of Eretum is just to the north, the city of Monterotondo is not mentioned in historical documents until the 11th century. In the Middle Ages the town and its fortress were properties of the Capocci and then Orisini families. In the 17th century the Barberini family acquired the town, and the grand Palazzo Orsini-Barberini still dominates its center, now serving as the town hall. The 17th-century Basilica of Santa Maria Maddelena faces the central street of the old city and on its ceiling are frescoes by Domenico Pistrini.

Now a bedroom community of Rome, Monterotondo bustles with people of all ages in the *passegiata* – the Italian evening stroll – either on a lower course that leads from Palazzo Orsini-Barberini downhill along the north side of Via Bruno Buozzi or on an upper course along the restaurants, pizzerias and *gelato* shops of the old city's Via Cavour, between the Basilica and Piazza dei Leoni.

La Cupella B&B (Via Vincenzo Bellini 36, tel 333 3489411, info@lacupella.it, €50/60) has a hip vibe and is located in the historic center. Right in the heart of the old city at Piazza dei Leoni is Albergo dei Leoni (Viale Federici 23, tel 0690 623591, info@albergodeileoni.it, €60/75) and its good restaurant. The Convento Frati Cappuccini (Piazza San Francesco, tel 0690 627534) also offers beds to pilgrims.

STAGE 27

Monterotondo to Monte Sacro

Start	Fausto Cecconi Memorial, Monterotondo
Finish	Chiesa Angelus Custodius, Monte Sacro
Distance	19.3km
Total ascent	711m
Total descent	422m
Difficulty	Easy
Duration	6hrs

The first half of the day is a refreshing walk through farmland, while the second half transitions into the busy and somewhat bleak suburbs of Rome where at least the path is easy to find, and bars, restaurants and *gelato* shops are plentiful.

Begin at the Fausto Cecconi Arch, and with the *passeggiata* route along Viale Bruno Buozzi behind you turn right onto Via Fausto Cecconi and walk uphill. ▶ Continue up the hill and just after the Chiesa di San Francesco on the left there is a fork in the road. Take the right fork that continues uphill. In 200m arrive at the summit and look ahead to the rolling hills between here and Rome.

Note the grocery store below and to the right in 100m.

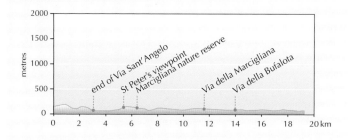

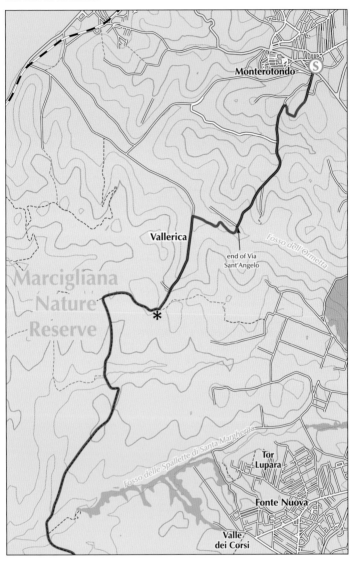

Walk downhill and in another 100m turn right onto Dei Frati Minori. In two blocks turn right on Dei Frati Crociferi, which veers downhill and to the left. You are now on Via Sant'Angelo, which you follow on a steep descent past vegetable gardens. In 500m come to the valley floor where you begin an uphill climb. The summit arrives in 500m and you go straight at a fork in the road. At another fork 300m later go straight again, walking downhill. In 600m go through the gate across the road and continue straight ahead.

Here there is a waymark sign that swivels randomly to the right or left. If the arrow is pointing right, turn it to face left.

Via Sant'Angelo ends in 100m at a 90-degree turn (3.1km). ▶ There is no outlet on the road to the right, so turning left, cross a gully onto an open field and immediately turn right onto a tractor road. Follow the tractor road as it makes a right turn past the bamboo hedge and continue on the road as it winds left then right, going toward the settlement of Vallericca ahead.

The tractor road comes to a home with a green gate. Go straight ahead, keeping the house and gate on the right. When this road ends in 100m turn left onto Via di Valle Ricca and continue on this long road uphill for 1.5km past an olive oil factory.

Pilgrims walking through fields outside Monterotondo

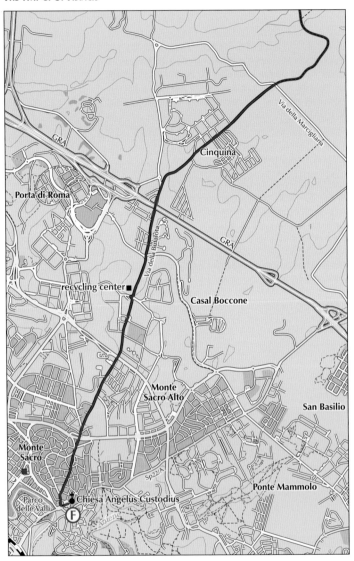

The road ends at a T-junction **viewpoint** where you can look straight ahead and on a clear day see the dome of St Peter's Basilica on the horizon. Turn right here and go through or around the 'Do Not Enter' gate. Follow this gravel road between houses for 900m and watch for the white, hand-lettered sign that directs you to turn left and downhill onto a gravel road toward open fields of the **Riserva Naturale delle Marcigliana** (6.3km).

Stay on this road through the vast preserve, made mostly of open, grassy fields. The road turns to asphalt in 1.8km after a climb. Continue straight for the next 3.7km until you come to a right fork and finally a stop sign at **Via della Marcigliana** (11.6km). Go straight at the stop sign, staying on Via di Tor San Giovanni, and leave the Italian countryside behind you as you enter the first suburbs of Rome.

The road now widens with sidewalks and turn lanes. Veer to the left in 2.6km as the road joins the busy **Via della Bufalota** (14km), which merges from the right and becomes your primary route into Monte Sacro. Follow this road under the freeway overpass (A90), cross the Via Settibagni and stay on the left or right side of the road – wherever the intermittent sidewalk is best. Pass directly in

Odd towers off Via della Bufolata

251

MONTE SACRO 40M POP 62,599

Chiesa dei Santi Angeli Custodi and Piazza Sempione, Monte Sacro

Monte Sacro is the 16th District of Rome, sitting on the far north-north-east edge of the metropolis. The name derives from the ancient sacrifices and auguries made at this low ridge above the Aniene River. The Ponte Nomentano across the Aniene was one of the strategic entries into Rome.

In the Plebian Revolt of 494BC, the lower classes took up residence at Monte Sacro in rebellion against the Patricians. During the Middle Ages the area was largely depopulated but with urbanization it was incorporated into metropolitan Rome, at first under the name Garden City and then under its new-old name, Monte Sacro in 1951.

The 20th-century Chiesa dei Angeli Custodi replaces an earlier building demolished in the late 1920s. Frescoes painted by Aaron del Vecchio in 1962 richly adorn the vault.

Right along the route is Domus Città Giardino B&B (Viale Adriatico 20, tel 0687 195387, info@domuscittagiardino.it, €50/60) where pilgrims are warmly welcomed. About 10 blocks away is Minerva Casa Vacanze e Studio (Via Conca d'Oro 300, tel 335 6694320, info@bbminervaroma.it, from €40/55). Just a couple of blocks after the Aniene River bridge is Casa Vacanze/Casa Pace (Via Nomentana 117, tel 349 0676760). Note that the Conca d'Oro Metro Line B is just a few blocks NW of the stage's end, making all of Rome's hotels and hostels easily accessible.

front of the **recycling center** and then cross to the opposite side to go through the traffic circle. Ahead you see a tall, three-legged concrete tower. Continue on Via della Bufalota past the tower.

Come to a summit and start walking under trees downhill into Monte Sacro, which is in Municipio III of Rome. The street now becomes the Viale Adriatico. ◀ Continue downhill and near the bottom veer left at the fork. The road now becomes Via Gargano. In 50m turn left at Via Nomentana and see the **Chiesa Angelus Custodius** ahead, the end of the stage.

Note the Città Giardino B&B on the left.

STAGE 28

Monte Sacro to Vatican City

Start	Chiesa Angelus Custodius, Monte Sacro
Finish	Saint Peter's Square, Vatican City
Distance	15.4km
Total ascent	158m
Total descent	168m
Difficulty	Easy
Duration	4hrs 30mins
Note	While it is easy enough to take the Metro from Monte Sacro to the Vatican, this route offers a quiet and enjoyable walk along the Aniene and Tiber Rivers before a climactic entry to Vatican City.

Today's stage avoids much of the noise and traffic of urban Rome by guiding you through parks, along rivers and on bike paths. St Peter's Basilica at the Vatican is the emotional climax of the walk. Services are available within a few blocks along the way, with pavement underfoot the entire distance until the splendor of Saint Peter's.

With your back to the Santi Angeli Custodi church, walk straight ahead along the Corso Sempione and cross the

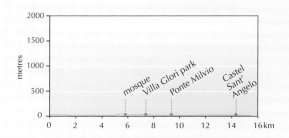

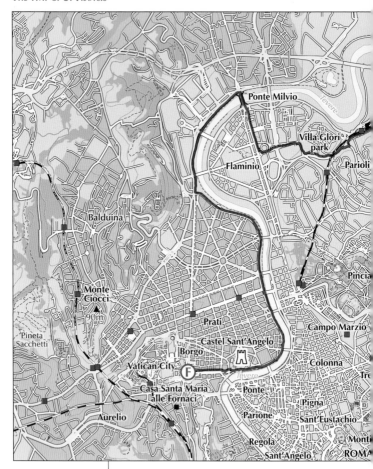

Viale Tirreno. Cross the Aniene River on the Ponte Tazio and immediately turn right onto the sidewalk. You will follow this sidewalk, which becomes a pleasant bike path, much of the way to the Vatican.

In 250m cross under railroad tracks, which accompany you for the next kilometer. The intersection of two

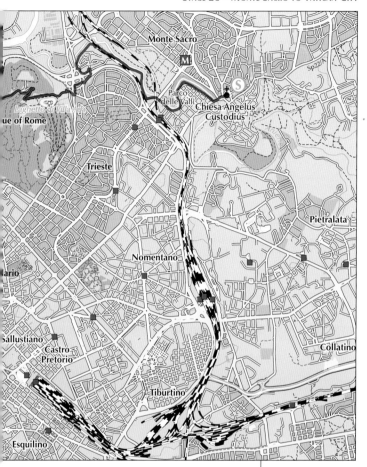

major highways, the Via Salaria (SS4) and the Via del Foro Italico, comes in 600m. Watch the waymarks very carefully and stay on the pink bike path to go around the complex cloverleaf exchange that crosses the Via Salaria. Finally on the other side, watch carefully for a path that leads on steps downhill to the left. Take this path past a parking lot to the right, and come to the entrance of the Villa Ada park.

Leave the park gate on your left and continue to the right along the Via di Ponte Salario as it winds its way uphill and down on switchbacks. In 1.3km you come to the Via di Moschea. Turn left and once again follow the pink bike trail, crossing the Via Anna Magnani with the **Mosque of Rome** on your right.

Pass the aqua fitness center on your left and after 1.3km you come to a T-junction. Cross the Via Francesco Densa then cross another street, turn right and go toward the **Villa Glori park**. You now arrive at the park entrance on your right (7.3km). ◄ You have come to the Viale Pilsudski, which you follow as it veers right along the park and its equestrian center.

Take the first right onto Via Giulio Galdini and then the first left onto Viale Pietro de Coubertin where you enter the Parco della Musica with its auditoriums on the left. Join the bike path again as it goes under the highway overpass to the left of the domed Palazzetto dello Sport. Turn right onto Via Tiziano, adjacent to a children's park and its giant red geometric sculpture.

Note that the park and neighborhood have several restaurants and bars.

Piazza San Pietro and façade of St Peter's Basilica

Continue on the bike path for 600m, past the Piazzale Cardinal Consalvi toward the pedestrian-only **Ponte Milvio** bridge (9.2km). Cross the bridge over the Tiber River – which has grown wide since you last saw it at Città di Castello – and turn left on the broad asphalt walk that follows just above the riverbank. In 600m look left for your first view of Castel Sant'Angelo and the dome of St Peter's Basilica.

After a time the trail rises up from the river and comes to an intersection. Turn left and stay on the bike path above the river. To your left is the first of nine bridges you will pass before arriving at the Vatican.

Continue on the bike path. In 1.7km pass a second bridge and, in 300m, come to an automobile and train bridge. Cross the road and tracks on the stairway and pedestrian bridge to its right. Follow the path for another 1.6km as you come to **Castel Sant'Angelo** on the right and the final bridge, Ponte Sant'Angelo on the left. Straight ahead at the end of Via della Conciliazione are St Peter's Square and St Peter's Basilica.

Congratulations – you have arrived at one of the great buildings of the world. You have stepped out of Italy into **Vatican City** and the culmination of your pilgrimage.

To enter St Peter's Basilica, join the queue for a security check. St Peter's offers a *timbro* to pilgrims in the basilica's Sacrestia, accessed through the left transept of the Basilica, upon presentation of a pilgrim credential.

After visiting the Basilica you may receive your completion certificate – your Testimonium – by going to the Polizia van outside and to the left of the Basilica where you will undergo a separate security check for entry into the secured section of the Vatican. The Vatican Polizia will direct you past the Swiss guards to the Vatican security office. Get an entry pass there and go along the Basilica wall to the Palazzo della Canonica on the left. Inside the building turn right and request your Testimonium from the person at the desk. On your way back out of the Vatican, return your entry pass to the security office.

VATICAN CITY 31M POP 842

St Peter's Basilica, completed in the 17th century, is the crown jewel of Vatican City, which is the capital of the Roman Catholic Church – a tiny and independent country in its own right and one of the most celebrated pilgrimage destinations in the world. The Vatican's 44 hectares hold the Vatican Museum and Library, which include unsurpassed collections of art and literature accumulated for the last 2000 years. The Vatican, of course, is home to the Pope, and from here he leads the church of some 1.2 billion adherents.

A tour of the Vatican begins within the 17th-century colonnade around Saint Peter's Square, designed by the sculptor Bernini. At the center is an ancient Egyptian obelisk (circa 2400BC) known as 'The Witness,' which originally stood at the Circus of Nero and is believed to have witnessed the crucifixion of St Peter. The vast square surrounds the obelisk and fountains, and atop the colonnade that rings the square are 96 statues of saints and martyrs.

Opening to the piazza are the doors of St Peter's Basilica, a marvel of architecture and one of the largest churches in the world. Rebuilt on the site of the fourth-century church of Constantine, which itself was built over the traditional site of St Peter's tomb, the building of the 'new' St Peter's spanned 120 years, beginning in 1506. Most famous of its architects was Michelangelo, who designed the massive dome that can be seen from throughout Rome. His 'Pieta' sculpture is on the right aisle of the nave.

Pilgrims often rub the foot of the bronze statue of St Peter by Cambio, also in the nave. For €7 it is possible to walk through the inside of the dome, 551 steps above to the cupola to enjoy its unparalleled view of Rome and its environs. Note that strict adherence to modesty is required in the Vatican, and bare shoulders and knees must be covered. It is wise to purchase the €16 tickets for the famed Vatican Museum and Sistine Chapel in advance at www.museivaticani.va.

Among the hundreds of options for lodging in Rome, two stand out. The delightful Spedale della Divina Provvidenza (Via dei Genovesi 11B, tel 3272 319312, info@pellegriniaroma.it, by donation, two nights maximum. A pilgrim credential and proof of walking the last 100km is required for entry. Reserve at least two days in advance) is run in part by the Italian Brotherhood of Santiago de Compostela, famous for the ceremony of pilgrim foot-washing. Just 10 minutes from the Vatican is Casa per Ferie Santa Maria alle Fornaci (Piazza Santa Maria alle Fornaci 27, tel 0639 367632, www.trinitaridematha.it, €50/55 includes breakfast) of the Trinitarian Order – a favorite among religious pilgrims.

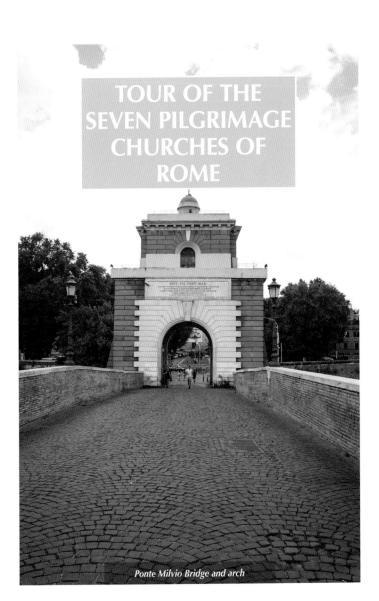

TOUR OF THE SEVEN PILGRIMAGE CHURCHES OF ROME

Ponte Milvio Bridge and arch

259

TOUR OF THE SEVEN PILGRIMAGE CHURCHES OF ROME

Start	Saint Peter's Basilica, Vatican City
Finish	Saint Paul's Basilica Outside the Walls, Rome
Distance	19.9km
Total ascent	237m
Total descent	235m
Difficulty	Easy
Duration	6hrs 30mins
Note	On Wednesdays the Catacombs of Callistus are closed, requiring a bus transfer to complete the walk safely.

For nearly 500 years pilgrims have visited the seven pilgrim churches of Rome as a spiritual discipline or to receive remission from their sins. This largely urban walk covers the four most important basilicas in Rome as well as three other important, historic churches. It is best to start around 7.00am since some of the churches close at noon and do not reopen until 3.30pm.

Standing in St Peter's Square with the **Basilica** behind you, go straight ahead on Via della Conciliazione toward Castel Sant'Angelo. At the castle turn right onto the bridge and cross the Tiber River.

After crossing go straight onto the Via del Bianco di Santo Spiritu. Before the stoplight take a half-left turn onto Via di Bianchi Nuovi, and in 150m come to the Piazza del Orologio. Go left of the building with the large clock tower and get onto the Via del Governo Vecchio.

In 400m you arrive at the Piazza di Pasquino. Cross the piazza, going straight ahead onto the Via di Pasquino, which takes you after one block to the south end of Piazza Navona. Cross the foot of the piazza, going straight ahead.

One block after the piazza turn right on Corso di Rinascimento. Walk toward the Basilica di San Andrea della Valle and turn left onto Corso Vittorio Emanuele II.

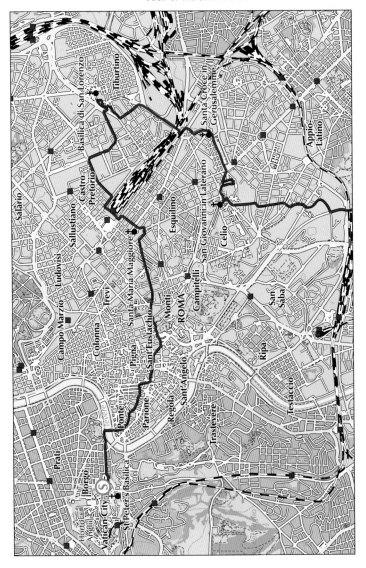

One block after the piazza turn right on Corso di Rinascimento. Walk toward the Basilica di San Andrea della Valle and turn left onto Corso Vittorio Emanuele II. Keep the Basilica on your right and follow Corso Vittorio Emanuel II for 400m until a fork at the Chiesa del Gesú. Take the right fork, keeping the church on your left.

One block later turn left on Via San Marco and follow this street, crossing the busy road to the front steps of the huge, white Vittorio Emanuele II Monument. With the steps of the monument on your right, look directly ahead to the first-century Colonna Traiana – a tall column topped by a 16th-century statue of St Peter – which is just to the left of the Trajan Forum ruins. Cross the busy street toward the column.

Continue past the column, keeping the Santissimo Nome di Maria church on your left and head up the wide stairway at the end of the lane. At the top of the stairs go straight ahead to the traffic circle, then veer right and follow the Via Panisperna past two churches as you climb the hill.

Basilica of Santa Maria Maggiore

Atop the hill at the second church, round the curve and at the end of the long road ahead you can now see **Santa Maria Maggiore**. Continue downhill and then uphill again toward the back corner of the church. Turn right and walk along Via Liberiana for one block until the piazza, where you can enter the front door of the church on your left (4.6km).

> Since the mid-fifth century a **church dedicated to the Virgin Mary** has stood at the site of the Basilica of Santa Maria Maggiore. Continually remodeled and expanded, the church is a center of Marian devotion and one of four official Papal Basilicas of Rome. The crypt contains what is venerated as a fragment of the manger of Bethlehem.
>
> Take note of the 36 columns of the nave, made of Athenian marble hewn of single blocks of stone. Above each column are scenes from the Old Testament. Of special note are the intricate fifth-century mosaics in the church's triumphal arch and the 13th-century mosaic by Torriti in the apse that depicts the coronation of Mary by her Divine Son.

Standing with the church at your back, turn left and cross the street onto the Via Gioberti. Walk three blocks ahead to the street's end at the large white Termini Station. Turn left at the station and a half block later turn right, entering the station itself. Cross through the building and turn right onto Via Marsala. Turn left two blocks later onto Via del Castro Pretorio and follow it through the stoplight until Viale delle Scienze, where you turn right.

Come to a fork in the road at the Consiglio Nazionale delle Ricerche and go left onto Via dei Marrucini. Two blocks later turn left onto Via Cesare de Lollis; from here you can see the **Basilica di San Lorenzo Fuori le Mura** straight ahead. Walk toward the transit center and, once there, carefully cross the busy street to the right. Walk across the Piazza di San Lorenzo, passing its obelisk, and come to the church (7.5km).

Before his martyrdom by the pagan Emperor Valerian in 258, Pope Sixtus instructed his treasurer, **Lorenzo**, to sell the possessions of the Roman church and give them to the poor. When imperial authorities arrested Lorenzo they commanded him to surrender the church's treasures; at the appointed time he brought to the authorities a throng of paupers and sickly beggars. Thinking he had tricked them, the Prefect ordered Lorenzo to be whipped and roasted to death over red-hot coals.

The Church of San Lorenzo Outside the Walls, dedicated to his memory, is actually a fourth- to sixth-century church, joined at the apse with a church built in the seventh century.

After your visit, stand facing the obelisk and look ahead to the statue of Pope Pius XII in the small park. Walk through the park and just after the statue turn left. Go a couple of small blocks toward a flower shop and turn right, walking slightly uphill on Piazzale dei Verano. Turn left on Via dei Rieti, following the tram tracks.

Interior of Basilica Santa Croce

In four blocks turn right onto Viale dell Scalo San Lorenzo with its overhead railroad bridge. Go straight ahead 700m and continue through a car and pedestrian underpass beneath the train tracks. You now come to Porta Maggiore.

At the stoplight turn left and go through the city walls. Turn right and go through another gate, then turn left, pass a large utility building on the left and continue on Via Eleniana as it curves toward the right in front of the **Basilica di Santa Croce in Gerusalemme** (9.8km).

> When Christianity was legalized in the Roman Empire, the Emperor Constantine's mother, **Helena**, commissioned Christian churches to be built in Jerusalem at sites that had been suppressed by Roman emperors. In the early stages of construction at the traditional site of Golgotha, a wooden plaque with the inscription 'INRI' was found, along with three crosses. The local bishop verified one of the crosses as the true cross of Jesus' crucifixion and Helena brought it to Rome as the centerpiece of her Church of Santa Croce in Gerusalemme, which dates from the fourth century.
>
> Inside the building to the left of the sanctuary is a door that leads past a piece of the cross of the Good Thief and then up a stairway to the Chapel of the Relics of the Passion, where pilgrims can view the plaque and other relics of the cross.

From the front door of the church take a half-left and now, through the long, tree-lined boulevard ahead you can catch a glimpse of the Basilica di San Giovanni in Laterano.

Enter the long park to the left of the boulevard and follow the path to the monument to San Francesco, which commemorates his visit there with Pope Innocent III on 16 April 1210. Directly across the busy street is the Lateran Church. Cross the street and go through the piazza to enter the front doors of the **Basilica di San Giovanni Laterano** (10.1km).

St John Lateran is built at the site of Rome's first Christian church, and as the cathedral church of the Bishop of Rome, the Pope, it is preeminent among all Roman churches.

Originally constructed at the order of Emperor Constantine in the early fourth century, it is one of four Papal Basilicas of Rome. Because of fires and earthquakes the church was reconstructed in the 10th century and was then rededicated to both St John the Evangelist and St John the Baptist. Of special note are the two central bronze doors at the entry, which originally served as entry portals to the ancient Roman Senate and were repurposed here following the Fall of Imperial Rome.

It was here at St John Lateran that Pope Innocent III interviewed Francis of Assisi. In a dream after the interview, Innocent saw the man in a brown robe holding up the pillars of the Lateran Church to keep it from falling in an earthquake. Innocent III soon approved the Franciscan order and served as protector of Francis in the first years of his ministry.

After leaving the church through its front door turn left. Take note of the church across the street, the Scala Santa Church, which houses the relocated steps traditionally associated with the trial of Jesus Christ by Pontius Pilate.

Go to the street and turn left again after the Lateran Palace. Continue ahead and cross the Piazza Giovanni Paolo II and its baptistery and follow the Via dell'Amba Aradam. Turn at the first left, the Via dei Laterani, and follow this road until its end at a brick wall. Turn right and then 30m later turn left onto the Via Illiria, which you follow slightly uphill under trees.

Continue until the Mercato Latino, which you pass on your left side. Here take a half-right turn onto the Via Aquitania between two residential buildings. Go straight ahead and see the city walls before you.

Turn left onto Viale Metronio at the city walls and follow this as it curves around the walls to the Porta Latina. Do not enter the gate, but instead continue to follow the city walls, now on the Viale dell Mure Latine as it turns hard right and comes to the ancient Porta San Sebastiano and Drusus Arch (dating from the third century), through which the famous Appian Way enters the city gates.

At the Porta San Sebastiano turn left onto Via Appia Antica. Continue on this ancient road through the double underpass for 900m to the Chiesa Quo Vadis, traditional site of the vision of Christ by St Peter that convinced him to return to Rome for his execution.

The church is at a fork in the road. Cross between the two forks into the Reservate Catacombe di San Callisto, an enormous park complex. (**Please note** that on Wednesdays the reserve is closed, so because the Via Appia Antica is treacherous for pedestrians in the next stretch it is advisable on those days to take the Mobilitá 118 bus instead.)

Continue 1.6km through the park, past its buildings, fields and along a modern Stations of the Cross. At the end of the drive, veer left toward the 'Uscita – Appia Antica' sign and follow the driveway downhill to the exit gate at the Via Appia Antica. Turn right, cross the street and walk 30m to the **Basilica di San Sebastiano Fuori le Mura** and its catacombs (15.7km).

The Interior of San Sebastiano

Outside Rome on the ancient Appian Way is an area known as 'The Hollows,' or *catacumbus* in Latin – an area used for subterranean burials. Many saints and martyrs had their burials here, and the initial resting places of the bodies of Saints Peter and Paul were here, as well as that of **St Sebastian**, a third-century martyr.

As a nobleman and prominent officer in the Roman army, Sebastian was horrified by the persecutions of Emperor Valerian. He smuggled Christians into hiding and ministered to those in prison. Soon he adopted the Christian faith as his own. Upon learning of his conversion, Valerian ordered Sebastian's execution by a firing squad of archers. Although many arrows pierced him, Sebastian survived and a second execution was ordered, after which the Emperor had his body thrown into the sewer. Reclaimed by Christian friends, his ashes were then buried in the catacombs and the church built on the site was dedicated in his honor.

The six granite columns of the portico are all that remain of the original fourth-century church; the remainder dates from the early 17th century. Many prominent pilgrims have visited the church's catacombs over the centuries, including Saints Jerome, Catherine of Sienna, Charles Borromeo, Philip Neri and others.

From the front door of the church return to Via Appia Antica and turn left, followed in 30m by another left onto the Vicolo delle Sette Chiese opposite the Callisto catacomb entrance. Follow this traditional pilgrim road as it becomes the Via delle Sette Chiese.

After 1km pass a park with a modern sculpture and then come to a large T-junction ahead. Turn left onto the Via Cristoforo Colombo, pass a gas station and cross the street at the stoplight. Go straight to the roundabout and take the second left back onto the Via delle Sette Chiese.

Basilica di San Paolo Fuori le Mura

After the traffic circle is a small park with a road on the right paved in cobblestones. Take this road and come to a small piazza and then a roundabout. Go straight, just to the right of a farmacia, still on the Via delle Sette Chiese. Continue past older homes and then the Catacombe di Commodilla on the left, continuing slightly uphill.

Soon you come to the top of a small rise and afterward you cross the Viale Leonard Da Vinci and then immediately the rail tracks on an overpass. The road turns left and you now can glimpse the **Basilica di San Paolo Fuori le Mura** on the left. Cross the Via Ostiense and reach the back corner of the Basilica. Turn right and follow the church wall around to the front portico (19.9km).

According to tradition, **St Paul** was beheaded two miles outside the Roman walls on the road to Ostia. Knowing this, three centuries later Emperor Constantine built a church in his honor at that location and moved his remains from the catacombs to the church site.

269

As it became one of the most popular pilgrimage destinations in Rome, the church was expanded over the centuries. In 1823 a fire in its rafters almost completely destroyed the structure, leaving only the great archway over the sanctuary and the apse. Artists and donors from around the world collaborated to recreate the building and its priceless mosaics, and the resulting building is said to be very close to its previous appearance. St Paul Outside the Walls (as it translates in English) is one of the Four Papal Basilicas of Rome.

Visitors walk through a colonnade and atrium surrounding the gardens in front of the Basilica's portico. At the end of the vast nave is the apse, with its 13th-century mosaic. Under the altar are the bones of St Paul, persecutor of the faith, who became Apostle to the Gentiles.

To return to the center of the city, turn left from the basilica front door and go to the stoplight. Turn left again and follow the road two long blocks to the Metro Station, just 200m away from the basilica at the Basilica San Paolo stop on Line B.

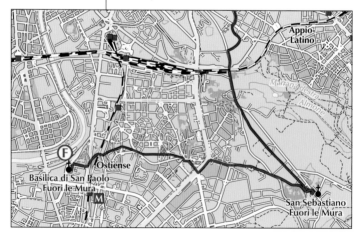

APPENDIX A

Route summary table

Stage no	From/To	Distance (km)	Climb (m)	Descent (m)	End-of-stage services			Page
					Train	Bus	Hostel or parish beds	
1	Firenze to Pontassieve	23.8	602	553				44
2	Pontassieve to Consuma	17.8	1021	138	Y	Y		53
3	Consuma to Stia	17	536	1093		Y	Y	59
4	Stia to Camaldoli	16.6	1017	583	Y	Y	Y	66
5	Camaldoli to Badia Prataglia	8.4	534	519		Y	Y	72
6	Badia Prataglia to La Verna	17.5	1194	959		Y	Y	77
7	La Verna to Pieve Santo Stefano	15.2	309	983		Y		88
8	Pieve S. Stefano to Sansepolcro	25	447	539	Y	Y	Y	94
9	Sansepolcro to Citerna	12.5	280	124		Y	Y	101
10	Citerna to Città di Castello	20.3	816	938	Y	Y	Y	106

Stage no	From/To	Distance (km)	Climb (m)	Descent (m)	End-of-stage services			Page
					Train	Bus	Hostel or parish beds	
11	Città di Castello to Pietralunga	29.8	889	607		Y	Y	114
12	Pietralunga to Gubbio	26.5	784	760		Y	Y	120
13	Gubbio to Biscina	22.7	895	688				129
14	Biscina to Valfabbrica	15.9	427	669		Y	Y	137
15	Valfabbrica to Assisi	13.4	530	456	Y	Y	Y	142
16	Assisi to Spello (easy)	13.8	301	429	Y	Y	Y	154
16a	Assisi to Spello (difficult)	17.6	925	1024	Y	Y	Y	159
17	Spello to Trevi	19.1	429	243	Y	Y	Y	167
18	Trevi to Spoleto	18.8	275	363	Y	Y	Y	175
19	Spoleto to Ceselli	15.3	641	663		Y	Y	183
20	Ceselli to Arrone	15.5	221	248		Y	Y	191
21	Arrone to Piediluco	14.5	294	152		Y	Y	196
22	Piediluco to Poggio Bustone	21.8	978	662		Y	Y	203

Stage no	From/To	Distance (km)	Climb (m)	Descent (m)	End-of-stage services			Page
					Train	Bus	Hostel or parish beds	
23	Poggio Bustone to Rieti	17.7	395	745	Y	Y	Y	211
24	Rieti to Poggio San Lorenzo	21.8	499	377		Y		222
25	Poggio San Lorenzo to Ponticelli	23.2	821	1015		Y	Y	229
26	Ponticelli to Monterotondo	29.8	690	871	Y	Y	Y	237
27	Monterotondo to Monte Sacro	19.3	711	422	Y	Y	Y	247
28	Monte Sacro to Vatican City	15.4	158	168	Y	Y	Y	253
Total: Florence to Rome		**528.4**						
Seven Pilgrim Churches		19.9	237	235	Y	Y		260

APPENDIX B
Useful contacts

Tourist information offices
Additional information on lodging and sites of interest can be requested at tourist information offices along the way. As Italian government agencies, these offices can provide information about commercial hotels and campgrounds, but not unlicensed parochial or private hostels.

Florence
There are five provincial tourist information offices, including at Vespucci Airport (tel 055 315874, infoaeroporto@firenzeturismo.it) and across from Santa Maria Novella Train Station (Piazza Stazione 4, tel055 212245, turismo3@comune.fi.it).

Pontassieve and Consuma
No tourist information offices

Stia
Municipal tourist office in nearby Pratovecchio (Piazza Maccioni 1, tel 0575 504877, anagrafe.pratovecchio@casentino.toscana.it)

Camaldoli Village
Tourist information office of the Casentino National Forest (tel 0575 556130, cv.camaldoli@parcoforestecasentinesi.it) with park ranger staff members, an ornithological museum, books and national forest maps.

Badia Prataglia
Tourism information office for the national forest (Via Nazionale 14a, tel 0575 559477, cv.badiaprataglia@parcoforestecasentinesi.it).

Santuario della Verna/Chiusi della Verna
No tourist information office.

Pieve Santo Stefano
No tourist information office

Sansepolcro
Tourism office of the Province of Arezzo, Valtiberina region (Via Matteotti 8, tel 0575 740536, info@valtiberinaintoscana.it)

Citerna
No tourist information office

Città di Castello
An office of the Umbria tourism department (Piazza Matteotti – Logge Bufalini, tel 0758 554922, info@iat.citta-di-castello.pg.it)

Pietralunga
A small municipal information office (Piazza Fiorucci 1, tel 0759 460721, commune@pietralunga.it)

Gubbio
A municipal tourism office combined with the Umbria tourist office (Via della Repubblica 15, tel 0759 220693 info@iat.gubbio.pg.it)

Biscina
No tourist information office

Assisi
Tourist information office of the Region of Umbria (Piazza del Comune, tel 0758 138680 info@iat.assisi.pg.it)

Spello
Municipal tourist information office (Piazza Matteotti 3, tel 0742 301009, info@prospello.it)

Foligno
Tourism information office of Region Umbria on its main pedestrian street (Corso Cavour 126, tel 0742 354459, info@iat.foligno.pg.it)

Trevi
Volunteer-run tourist information office off Piazza Mazzini (Villa Fabri, tel 0742 332269, infoturismo@comune.trevi.pg.it)

Spoleto
Piazza della Libertà 7, tel 0743 218620, info@iat.spoleto.pg.it

Ceselli, Arrone and Poggio Bustone
No tourist information offices

Rieti
Municipal tourist information office in its city hall (Piazza Vittorio Emanuele II, tel 0746 488537, turismo@comune.rieti.it) and a tourist information office nearby for the Region of Lazio (rieti@visitlazio.com)

Poggio San Lorenzo and Ponticelli
No tourist information offices

Monterotondo
Tourist information near the city hall (Piazza Libertá 30, tel 069 066683, prolocomonterotondo@libero.it) as well as a small, staffed kiosk on the passeggiata (Viale Buozzi, tel 069 0622552)

Monte Sacro
No tourist information office

Rome
Rome has many large and small tourist offices. The main office is near the Repubblica Metro Station (Via Parigi 5, tel 060 60608, turismo@comune.roma.it). Smaller offices are near transportation centers like Fiumicino airport (Terminal 3) and Termini train station (Track 24, Via Giovanni Giolitti 34). In the historic center there are offices on Via Marco Minghetti (near the Piazza Venezia), near Piazza Navona (on Piazza delle Cinque Lune), near Castel Sant'Angelo (Piazza Pia) and near Santa Maria Maggiore (Via dell'Olmata).

Public transport websites

Bus
Tuscany
www.etruriamobilita.it

Umbria
www.umbriamobilita.it

Lazio
www.cotralspa.it

Rieti area
www.asmrieti.it

Train
Tren Italia (national train system)
www.trenitalia

TFT (Upper Arno Valley system)
www.trasportoferroviariotoscano.it

Umbria Mobilita
www.umbriamobilitia.it/it/orari/
servizio-ferroviario

CAI and GPX
CAI (Club Alpino Italiano)
www.cai.it

Open Cycle Maps
www.opencyclemap.org

Smartphone App with Open Cycle Map
www.viewranger.com

Commercial download of Open Cycle Maps
www.opencyclemap.org/collections

Pilgrim credential
Via di Francesco *credenziale*
www.viadifrancesco.it/credenziale-e-testimonium-viae-francisci/
(or email info@viadifrancesco.it)

Italian language resources
Italian grammar and vocabulary
www.italian.about.com

Smartphone app for learning Italian
www.duolingo.com

Commercial travel agencies
Via di Francesco-focused travel agency
www.ilmestierediviaggiare.it
(Italian and English)

Italy walking tours, including St Francis itineraries
www.girasole.com

Websites for other major St Francis pilgrim routes
Cammino di Assisi
www.camminodiassisi.it/EN (English)

Di Qui Passo San Francesco
www.diquipassofrancesco.it/En (English)

Via di Francesco
www.viadifrancesco.it (Italian)

St Francis Sacred Valley (Rieti area)
www.camminodifrancesco.it (Italian and English)

Franciscan Trail (Diocese of Gubbio)
www.ilsentierodifrancesco.it (Italian)

Emergency telephone numbers
Remember always to use the Italian country code (39) if you are calling from a non-Italian number

Telephone directory assistance	12
Carabinieri (national police)	112
Emergency police, ambulance and fire services	113
Fire department	115
Italian Automobile Club roadside assistance	116
Medical emergencies (ambulance)	118
Forest Fire Service	1515

APPENDIX C
Language tips

English is commonly spoken in the tourist cities of Italy, but the opposite is true in rural areas. Here are some pronunciation tips and sample phrases that might help for those times when sign language won't do.

Italian pronunciation guide

Vowels	Sound	Example
a	Like 'a' in 'father'	*mamma*
e	Like 'a' in 'say'	*sera*
i	Like 'e' in 'meet'	*amico*
o	Like 'o' in 'post'	*sole*
u	Like 'oo' in 'food'	*uno*

Single consonant	Sound	Example
c	c – before an 'i' or 'e' always sounds like 'ch' in 'church'	*ciao*
c	c – unless before 'i' or 'e' like 'k'	*casa*
g	g – before 'i' or 'e' like 'g' in 'general'	*giorno*
g	g – always like 'g' in 'goal' unless before 'i' or 'e'	*gusto*
h	h – always silent	*hotel*
r	r – rolled like 'r' in Spanish	*Roma*
z	z – like 'ts' in 'cats'	*grazie*

Combined consonants	Sound	Example
ch	like 'k'	*anche*
gh	like 'g' in 'goal'	*spaghetti*
gli	like 'lli' in 'million'	*figlio*
gn	like 'nyuh' in 'canyon'	*gnocchi*
sc	before 'i' or 'e' like 'sh' in 'shut'	*pesce*
sc	like 'sk' in 'skip' unless before 'i' or 'e'	*scala*

Unlike English, Italian pronunciation is very regular. If you follow these rules you'll be able to pronounce most all words.

Here are some basic useful phrases:

English	Italian
Good morning (or good day)	*Buongiorno*
Thank you	*Grazie*
Thank you very much	*Grazie tante*
You're welcome	*Prego*
Please	*Per favore*
Yes	*Sì*
No	*No*
Excuse me	*Mi scusi*
I'm sorry	*Mi dispiace*
I don't understand	*Non capisco*
I don't speak Italian	*Non parlo italiano*
I don't speak Italian very well	*Non parlo molto bene italiano*
Do you speak English?	*Parla inglese?*
Speak slowly, please	*Parli piano, per favore*
Repeat, please	*Ripeta, per favore*
What's your name?	*Come si chiama?*
My name is…	*Il mil nome é*
How are you?	*Come va?*
Do you speak English?	*Parla inglese?*
Where is the subway?	*Dov'è la metropolitana?*
Is the tip included?	*Il servizio è incluso?*
How much does that cost? (sg/pl)	*Quanto costa/costano?*
Do you have Wi-Fi?	*Avete Wi-Fi? (pronounced as in English)*
What is the password?	*Qual é la chiave?*
Can you help me?	*Mi può aiutare?*
Where is the bathroom?	*Dov'è la toilette?*

English	Italian
I would like to make a reservation	*Vorrei fare una prenotazione*
...for tonight	*...per stasera*
...for tomorrow night	*...per domani sera*
...for a single room	*...per una camera singola*
...for a double room	*... per una camera doppia*
...with a double bed	*... con un letto matrimoniale*
May I have a pilgrim stamp?	*Posso avere un timbro pellegrino?*
Is there a laundromat nearby?	*C'é una lavanderia nelle vicinanze?*
Do you have a laundry service?	*Avete un servizio di lavanderia?*
Is breakfast included?	*La colazione é inclusa?*
What time does the restaurant open?	*A che ora il ristorante aperto?*
What is the local specialty?	*Qual é la specialitá locale?*
May I have the check?	*Potrei avere il conto?*
I would like...	*Vorrei...*
Good evening	*Buonasera*
Good night	*Buonanotte*

APPENDIX D
Further reading

Autobiography and biography

Francis of Assisi and Clare of Assisi, *Francis and Clare: The Complete Works* (trans Regis Armstrong OFM, CAP & Ignatius Brady OFM), Paulist Press, 1982. A compendium of all writings of these two beloved children of Assisi.

Saint Bonaventure, *The Life of St Francis of Assisi* (TAN Edition), St Benedict Press, 2010. Authoritative in the early days.

Thomas of Celano, *The First Life of St Francis*, SFPCK, 2000. The most influential of the historical biographies.

G K Chesterton, *St Francis of Assisi*, Hodder and Stoughton, 1923. A brief and inspirational biography.

Father Omer Engelbert, *St Francis of Assisi: A Biography*, Franciscan Herald Press, 1965. The most comprehensive, authoritative and readable of the hundreds of biographies.

Adrian House, *Francis of Assisi: A Revolutionary Life*, Hidden Spring, 2001. Modern and fact-filled, but quite readable. A little sceptical, but also reverent.

E Gurney Salter, *The Legend of Saint Francis by the Three Companions*, Forgotten Books, 2012. Attributed to Brothers Leo, Rufino and Angelo as the first biography of Francis, written by witnesses to his life.

The Little Flowers of Saint Francis, Okey, trans, Dover, 2003. A classic collection of St Francis' sayings and legends, gathered by his followers.

Fiction

Nikos Kazantzakis, *Saint Francis* (trans P A Bien), Loyola Classics, 2005. As only Kazantzakis could, this fictionalized biography describes the inner turmoil of the holy man.

Joan Mueller, *Francis, the Saint of Assisi: A Novel*, New City Press, 2010. A novelized biography by a professor of theology and Christian spirituality.

Modern spiritual lessons

Richard Rohr OFM, *Eager to Love: The Alternative Way of Francis of Assisi*, Franciscan Media, 2014. This prominent and beloved author and Franciscan priest proposes a Franciscan model for a new mysticism.

John Sweeney, *The St Francis Prayer Book: A Guide to Deepen Your Spiritual Life*, Paraclete Press, 2004. A basic introduction to Franciscan spirituality.

Other guidebooks

Linda Bird Francke, *On the Road with Francis of Assisi: A Timeless Journey Through Umbria and Tuscany, and Beyond*, Random House, 2005. Reflections on St Francis' life and journeys.

Frank J Korn, *A Catholic's Guide to Rome: Discovering the Soul of the Eternal City*, Paulist Press, 2000. An extremely helpful guide to the historic sites of Christian Rome.

Roch Niemier OFM, *In the Footsteps of Francis and Clare*, St Anthony Messenger Press, 1999. A devotional guide to sites around Assisi, including stories of Francis and Clare.

Angela Maria Seracchioli, *On the Road with Saint Francis*, Terre di Mezzo Editore, 2013. A guide to Franciscan sites with rich details from the life of St Francis by a pilgrim pioneer. Details the Di Qui Passo itinerary from La Verna to Poggio Bustone.

Lucinda Vardey, *Traveling with the Saints in Italy: Contemporary Pilgrimages on Ancient Paths*, Castle Quay Books, 2005. Organized by region, this comprehensive guide details the biography, beliefs and pilgrim sites pertaining to Italy's most notable saints.

NOTES

NOTES

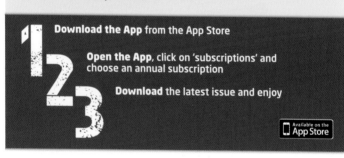

LISTING OF CICERONE GUIDES

The Southern Fells
The Western Fells
Roads and Tracks of the
  Lake District
Rocky Rambler's Wild Walks
Scrambles in the Lake District
  North & South
Short Walks in Lakeland
  1 South Lakeland
  2 North Lakeland
  3 West Lakeland
The Cumbria Coastal Way
The Cumbria Way
Tour of the Lake District

**DERBYSHIRE, PEAK DISTRICT
AND MIDLANDS**
High Peak Walks
Scrambles in the Dark Peak
The Star Family Walks
Walking in Derbyshire
White Peak Walks
  The Northern Dales
  The Southern Dales

SOUTHERN ENGLAND
Suffolk Coast & Heaths Walks
The Cotswold Way
The Great Stones Way
The Lea Valley Walk
The North Downs Way
The Peddars Way and Norfolk
  Coast Path
The Ridgeway National Trail
The South Downs Way
The South West Coast Path
The Thames Path
The Two Moors Way
Walking in Cornwall
Walking in Essex
Walking in Kent
Walking in Norfolk
Walking in Sussex
Walking in the Chilterns
Walking in the Cotswolds
Walking in the Isles of Scilly
Walking in the New Forest
Walking in the Thames Valley
Walking on Dartmoor
Walking on Guernsey
Walking on Jersey
Walking on the Isle of Wight
Walking on the North Wessex
  Downs
Walks in the South Downs
  National Park

WALES AND WELSH BORDERS
Glyndwr's Way
Great Mountain Days
  in Snowdonia
Hillwalking in Snowdonia
Hillwalking in Wales: 1&2
Offa's Dyke Path
Ridges of Snowdonia
Scrambles in Snowdonia
The Ascent of Snowdon
The Ceredigion and Snowdonia
  Coast Paths
Lleyn Peninsula Coastal Path
Pembrokeshire Coastal Path
The Severn Way
The Shropshire Hills
The Wales Coast Path
The Wye Valley Walk
Walking in Pembrokeshire
Walking in the Forest of Dean
Walking in the South Wales Valleys
Walking in the Wye Valley
Walking on Gower
Walking on the Brecon Beacons
Welsh Winter Climbs

**INTERNATIONAL CHALLENGES,
COLLECTIONS AND ACTIVITIES**
Canyoning
Canyoning in the Alps
Europe's High Points
The Via Francigena: 1&2

EUROPEAN CYCLING
Cycle Touring in France
Cycle Touring in Ireland
Cycle Touring in Spain
Cycle Touring in Switzerland
Cycling in the French Alps
Cycling the Canal du Midi
Cycling the River Loire
The Danube Cycleway Vol 1
The Grand Traverse of the
  Massif Central
The Moselle Cycle Route
The Rhine Cycle Route
The Way of St James

AFRICA
Climbing in the Moroccan
  Anti-Atlas
Kilimanjaro
Mountaineering in the Moroccan
  High Atlas
The High Atlas
Trekking in the Atlas Mountains
Walking in the Drakensberg

ALPS – CROSS-BORDER ROUTES
100 Hut Walks in the Alps
Across the Eastern Alps: E5
Alpine Points of View
Alpine Ski Mountaineering
  1 Western Alps
  2 Central and Eastern Alps
Chamonix to Zermatt
Snowshoeing
Tour of Mont Blanc
Tour of the Matterhorn
Trekking in the Alps
Trekking in the Silvretta and
  Rätikon Alps
Walking in the Alps
Walks and Treks in the
  Maritime Alps

**PYRENEES AND FRANCE/SPAIN
CROSS-BORDER ROUTES**
The GR10 Trail
The GR11 Trail – La Senda
The Mountains of Andorra
The Pyrenean Haute Route
The Pyrenees
The Way of St James:
  France & Spain
Walks and Climbs in the Pyrenees

AUSTRIA
The Adlerweg
Trekking in Austria's Hohe Tauern
Trekking in the Stubai Alps
Trekking in the Zillertal Alps
Walking in Austria

BELGIUM AND LUXEMBOURG
Walking in the Ardennes

EASTERN EUROPE
The High Tatras
The Mountains of Romania
Walking in Bulgaria's
  National Parks
Walking in Hungary

FRANCE
Chamonix Mountain Adventures
Ecrins National Park
Mont Blanc Walks
Mountain Adventures in
  the Maurienne
The Cathar Way
The GR20 Corsica
The GR5 Trail
The Robert Louis Stevenson Trail
Tour of the Oisans: The GR54

For full information on all our
guides, books and eBooks,
visit our website:
www.cicerone.co.uk.

Walking – Trekking – Mountaineering – Climbing – Cycling

Over 40 years, Cicerone have built up an outstanding collection of over 300 guides, inspiring all sorts of amazing adventures.

Every guide comes from extensive exploration and research by our expert authors, all with a passion for their subjects. They are frequently praised, endorsed and used by clubs, instructors and outdoor organisations.

All our titles can now be bought as **e-books**, **ePubs** and **Kindle** files and we also have an online magazine – **Cicerone Extra** – with features to help cyclists, climbers, walkers and trekkers choose their next adventure, at home or abroad.

Our website shows any **new information** we've had in since a book was published. Please do let us know if you find anything has changed, so that we can publish the latest details. On our **website** you'll also find great ideas and lots of detailed information about what's inside every guide and you can buy **individual routes** from many of them online.

It's easy to keep in touch with what's going on at Cicerone by getting our monthly **free e-newsletter**, which is full of offers, competitions, up-to-date information and topical articles. You can subscribe on our home page and also follow us on **Facebook** and **Twitter** or dip into our **blog**.

Cicerone – the very best guides for exploring the world.

CICERONE

2 Police Square Milnthorpe Cumbria LA7 7PY
Tel: 015395 62069 info@cicerone.co.uk
www.cicerone.co.uk and **www.cicerone-extra.com**